UNLOCKING THE MLA CODE

A textbook with excercises and worksheets

UPDATED

Gloria Dumler & David Moton

Onzième Edition
PUBLISHING COMPANY

Onzième Edition
PUBLISHING COMPANY

Copyright © 2018 by Gloria Dumler and David Moton
Cover designed by Adel Shafik

Published by Onzième Edition.
http://www.onzieme11edition.com

ISBN 978-0-9995740-8-9

Onzième Edition is a registered trademark of Onzième Edition Publishing Company.

All rights reserved. No part of this publication may be reproduced, stored in a retrieval system, or transmitted, in any form or by any means, electronic, mechanical, photocopying, recording, or otherwise, without the prior permission of the copyright owner.

Inquiries: www.onzieme11edition.com

Printing number: 9 8 7 6 5 4 3 2 1

Printed in the United States of America

CONTENTS

PREFACE	**XIII**
Note to Instructors	xiii
Note to Students	xiv
Book Contents	xvi

PART ONE	**1**
Document Format and Layout	
Document Layout	1
General Appearance of Papers	2
First Page	2
Personal and Class Identification Heading	3
Header	3
Title	4
Italics Versus Quotation Marks	5
Italics vs. Quotation Marks	6
The Wonderfully Boring History of Italics	7
Numbers in MLA Papers	7
Dates in MLA Papers	8
Potential Problems in Word Processing Programs	8

◀ Contents ▶

PART TWO 11

Parenthetical Citations

When to Use Parenthetical Citations 12
List of Parenthetical Citation Rules 12
What Goes Inside Parenthetical Citations? 13

1. One Author 13
2. Two Authors 13
3. Three or More Authors... 14
4. No Author 14
5. Page Numbers 14
6. No Page Numbers Listed.. 14
7. Format for Direct Quotations Four Lines or Less 15
8. Long/Block Quotations.. 15
9. Placement of Parenthetical In-Text Citations........................... 15
10. Quoted Material, Source Named Before Quotation 16
11. Comma and Colon Use 16
12. Quoted Material from an Electronic Source with No Author or Page Number Given 17
13. Same Source Used More than Once in One Paragraph............ 17
14. Quoted Material that Spans Two Pages..................................... 18
15. Corporate Authors, including Government Agencies 18
16. Paragraph Numbers in Citations 19
17. In-Text Citations for eBooks 19
18. Commonly-Studied Works in Multiple Editions 19
19. Sources Quoting Other Works 20
20. More than One Work by the Same Author............................... 20
21. Two or More Authors with the Same Last Name 21
22. Information from More than One Source 21
23. Citations for Films, Videos, and Lectures 21
24. Works in Time-Based Media 22
25. Translations of Quotations 22

◄ Contents ►

PART THREE   23

Works Cited Pages

Types of Works Cited Entries. 24

Common Features 24

   1. Basic Rules for MLA Works Cited Pages 26

   2. Core Elements Templates 28

   3. Determining Alphabetical Order 31

Books and Plays 32

   4. Identifying and Naming Publishers 32

   5. Cities of Publication 34

Basic Forms for Books and Plays 34

   6. Print Versions 34

   7. Book or Play with One Author 34

   8. Book or Play with Two Authors 35

   9. Book or Play with Three or More Authors 35

  10. Book with No Author Given 35

  11. eBook from an Internet Provider, Non-Subscription Service 36

  12. eBook from a Library Subscription Collection 36

  13. Translators 37

  14. Other Common Contributors 37

  15. Multiple Works by the Same Authors 37

  16. Pseudonyms 38

  17. Works by Corporate Authors, including Government Agencies ... 38

  18. A Single Article, Essay, or Other Work in a
      Collection or Anthology 40

  19. Multiple Selections from a Collection or Anthology
      (Cross-References) 40

  20. Introductions, Prefaces, Forewords, and Afterwords 41

  21. Article from a Multi-Volume Reference Set 42

  22. Graphic Novels and Comic Books 42

◀ Contents ▶

Periodicals: Scholarly Journals, Magazines, and Newspapers 43
   23. Basic Forms for Works from Periodicals 43
Scholarly Journals 45
   24. A Scholarly Journal Article in Print 45
   25. A Scholarly Journal Article from an Online Scholarly Journal 46
   26. A Scholarly Journal Article from a Library's Database 47
Magazines and Newspapers 48
   27. A Magazine Article in Print 48
   28. A Newspaper Article in Print 48
   29. A Newspaper Article or Book Review Published Online 49
   30. An Interview in a Newspaper or Magazine Published Online 50
Websites 51
   31. Article on a Collaborative Project's Website 51
   32. Authorless Article on an Organization's Website 51
   33. Web Project as a Whole 52
   34. Blogs and Blog Comments 52
   35. YouTube and Other Online Videos 53
Film, Television, DVDs, and Radio 54
   36. Feature Films and Documentaries 54
   37. Television Series, Individual Episodes, and Interviews 55
   38. Episodes in DVD sets 56
   39. Radio Programs 57
Other Sources 58
   40. Interviews, Lectures, and Public Addresses 58
   41. Advertisements 58
   42. Tweets 60
   43. Songs 60
   44. Slide-Based Presentations 61
   45. Artworks and Objects 61

◄ Contents ►

PART FOUR — 63

Writing Logical and Effective Argumentative Papers

Types of Papers 63
Thesis Statements 64
Debatable Thesis Statements 65
Narrowing Thesis Statements 66
Ethos, Logos, and Pathos 67
Audience 72
Structure and Organization 73
Basic Paper Guidelines 77
Section One: Thesis Statements 77
Section Two: Audience 78
Section Three: Sources, Evidence, and Support 78
Section Four: Proper Attribution of Ideas 79
Section Five: Use of Quotations 82
Section Six: Editing and Proofreading 83
Typical College Paper Grading Rubric 85
Annotated Sample Student Paper 88
Avoiding Faulty Arguments 105
Formal Fallacies 105
Informal Fallacies 106
Common Informal Fallacies 107

PART FIVE — 115

Understanding & Avoiding Plagiarism

Understanding and Avoiding Plagiarism 115
Types of Plagiarism 115
Rules for Avoiding Plagiarism 117

Examples of Plagiarized and Unplagiarized Paragraphs 119
Common Knowledge Exceptions 121

PART SIX   123

Brief Guide To Punctuation & Grammar

Important Elements of Punctuation and Grammar 123
Parts of Speech 123
    Nouns 123
    Pronouns 123
    Verbs 123
    Adjectives 124
    Adverbs 124
    Common Conjunctive Adverbs 124
    Conjunctions 124
    Coordinating Conjunctions 125
    Subordinating Conjunctions 125
    Prepositions 125
    Interjections 126
Building Grammatical Sentences 126
Recognizing and Punctuating Independent (Main) Clauses 128
Recognizing and Punctuating Dependent (Subordinate) Clauses 130
Basic Sentence Combining 131
Common Sentence Combining Errors to Avoid 132
    1. Comma splices 132
    2. Run-on sentences 132
    3. Sentence fragments 133
Recognizing and Punctuating Restrictive and Nonrestrictive Elements 134
    Other Uses of Commas 135
    Using Semicolons 138

◀ Contents ▶

Using Colons 139
Using Apostrophes 140
Using Quotation Marks 141
Using Terminal Punctuation Marks 142
Using Question Marks 142
Using Ellipsis Marks 143
Using Brackets 144

PART SEVEN   **147**

Practice Exercises And Keys
MLA Works Cited Practice Exercises and Keys **149**
WORKS CITED EXERCISE #1: A Book by One Author 149
WORKS CITED EXERCISE #2: Two Books by One Author 149
WORKS CITED EXERCISE #3: Two Books by Two Authors 149
WORKS CITED EXERCISE #4: One Book by Four Authors 150
WORKS CITED EXERCISE #5: eBook and Kindle Book 150
WORKS CITED EXERCISE #6: One Work from an Anthology 150
WORKS CITED EXERCISE #7: Multiple Works from the
    Same Anthology 150
WORKS CITED EXERCISE #8: Two Works from the Same Anthology
    and One Work from a Separate Anthology. 151
WORKS CITED EXERCISE #9: Two Works from Scholarly
    Journals: Print and Database 151
WORKS CITED EXERCISE #10: Two Works from Scholarly Journals:
    Database and Online-Only 152
WORKS CITED EXERCISE #11: Three Works from Magazines:
    Print, Database, and Online 152
WORKS CITED EXERCISE #12: Three Works from Newspapers:
    Print, Database, and Online 153
WORKS CITED EXERCISE #13: Articles on Websites 153

◀ Contents ▶

Works Cited Exercise #14: A Feature Film and a Documentary 154
Works Cited Exercise #15: A YouTube Video and a
Series on Netflix 154

Keys To The Exercises

Works Cited Exercise #1 Key: A Book by One Author 155
Works Cited Exercise #2 Key: Two Books by One Author 155
Works Cited Exercise #3 Key: Two Books by Two Authors 156
Works Cited Exercise #4 Key: One Book by Four Authors................. 157
Works Cited Exercise #5 Key: Ebook and Kindle Book 158
Works Cited Exercise #6 Key: One Work from an Anthology............ 158
Works Cited Exercise #7 Key: Two Works from
the Same Anthology 159
Works Cited Exercise #8 Key: Two Works from the Same Anthology
and One Work from a Separate Anthology. 160
Works Cited Exercise #9 Key: Two Works from Scholarly Journals:
Print and Database 161
Works Cited Exercise #10 Key: Two Works from Scholarly Journals:
Database and Online-Only.. 162
Works Cited Exercise #11 Key: Three Works from Magazines: Print,
Database, and Online 163
Works Cited Exercise #12 Key: Three Works from Newspapers: Print,
Database, and Online 164
Works Cited Exercise #13 Key: Articles on Websites 166
Works Cited Exercise #14 Key: A Feature Film and a Documentary..... 167
Works Cited Exercise #15 Key: A Youtube Video and a Series
on Netflix 168

PART EIGHT   171

Worksheets

Worksheet 1: MLA Page Layout Exercise #1 173

◀ Contents ▶

Worksheet 2:	MLA Page Layout Exercise #2	174
Worksheet 3:	MLA Page Layout Exercise #3	175
Worksheet 4:	MLA Page Layout Exercise #4	176
Worksheet 5:	MLA Page Layout Questions	177
Worksheet 6:	Parentheticals In-Text Citations Questions	179
Worksheet 7:	Parentheticals In-Text Exercise #1	181
Worksheet 8:	Parentheticals In-Text Exercise #2	182
Worksheet 9:	Parentheticals In-Text Exercise #3	183
Worksheet 10:	Works Cited Questions #1	185
Worksheet 11:	Works Cited Questions #2	187
Worksheet 12:	Works Cited Questions #3	189
Worksheet 13:	Works Cited Entries #1	191
Worksheet 14:	Works Cited Entries #2	192
Worksheet 15:	Works Cited Entries #3	193
Worksheet 16:	Works Cited Entries #4	194
Worksheet 17:	Works Cited Entries #5	195
Worksheet 18:	Works Cited Entries #6	196
Worksheet 19:	Sentence Combining Exercise #1	197
Worksheet 20:	Sentence Combining Exercise #2	200
Worksheet 21:	Punctuating Independent Clauses, Dependent Clauses, and Phrases	203
Worksheet 22:	Punctuating Nonrestrictive Elements	206
Worksheet 23:	Commas, Semicolons, Colons, and Periods Exercise #1	209
Worksheet 24:	Commas, Semicolons, Colons, and Periods Exercise #2	211
Worksheet 25:	Commas, Semicolons, Colons, and Periods Exercise #3	213
Worksheet 26:	Commas, Semicolons, Colons, and Periods Exercise #4	215
Worksheet 27:	Commas, Semicolons, Colons, and Periods Exercise #5	217
Worksheet 28:	Commas, Semicolons, Colons, and Periods Exercise #6	219
Worksheet 29:	Commas, Semicolons, Colons, and Periods Exercise #7	221
Worksheet 30:	Commas, Semicolons, Colons, and Periods Exercise #8	224

◀ Contents ▶

WORKSHEET 31:   Commas, Semicolons, Colons, and Periods Exercise #9 . 227
WORKSHEET 32:   Apostrophes, Plurals, and Pronouns Exercise #1 229
WORKSHEET 33:   Apostrophes, Plurals, and Pronouns Exercise #2 231
WORKSHEET 34:   Apostrophes, Plurals, and Pronouns Exercise #3 233
WORKSHEET 35:   Apostrophes, Plurals, and Pronouns Exercise #4 235

STUDENT NOTES   **237**

PREFACE

 NOTE TO INSTRUCTORS

This book is a student-friendly guide to the major elements and variations in the 8th edition of *The MLA Handbook*, the Modern Language Association's guide to documentation format. The "student-friendly" aspect is the most important part. We, the writers, are two college professors who have been teaching English for many years, and we believe that we have developed a feel for the difficulties that students face when trying to master these skills. In 2016, the Modern Language Association proclaimed about its revised guide, "The eighth edition of *The MLA Handbook* introduces a new model for entries in the works-cited list... In the new model, the work's publication format is not considered...the writer creates an entry by consulting the MLA's list of core elements."

These core elements contain terms like "location" and "container," and the committee who produced the eighth edition described the new approach as "intuitive." Frankly, we have found students more baffled than ever before. They are now asked to create works cited entries by combining what might be a series of more than one "container" into a single entry and figuring out that a "location" can mean any number of different kinds of components, including page numbers and websites. Even the punctuation marks in works cited entries have been changed to fit the new approach. Learning MLA format has always been challenging for many students, but now they feel like they are being asked to decipher a new code. We want to help them to unlock that code.

Unlocking the MLA Code starts with sections covering the basics of paper layout, parenthetical citations, works cited pages, writing logical and effective argumentative papers, and how to avoid plagiarism. We follow the first five parts with a concise guide to punctuation and grammar basics, focusing on practical guidelines and avoiding any jargon that students really do not need to know to write grammatical and well-punctuated sentences at the collegiate level.

◀ Preface ▶

The seventh part of the text consists of works cited practice exercises and keys that students can study on their own (the preparation of such entries may be the most challenging aspect of MLA format for students). The eighth part of the text is a series of worksheets for students to complete and turn in. We have tried to include a variety of worksheets that can be used as individual homework exercises, in-class work, group work, and quizzes. While the worksheets are designed to be torn out and turned in, they are located at the end of the book so that students will still have a usable guide they can use as a reference to help them through future classes. We have aimed to write the book in a voice that is as engaging and student-friendly as we can to make learning the rules and variations included in the new format less intimidating and to help students unlock the MLA code.

 NOTE TO STUDENTS

Imagine you were given a map by a mysterious relative. This map is supposed to lead you to a chest full of gold that was buried by a crazy great-grand-uncle of yours before the Great Depression. You get so excited at the prospect of paying off student loans and buying a new car with your new gold wealth, you can barely unroll the map without your hands shaking. Somehow, you manage it, and you spread it out on your cluttered desk. You see a dotted line leading through a wild landscape and eventually landing on an X, which marks the spot of the family treasure. However, the dotted line itself is confusing. It shows you should turn left, but the symbol that tells you where to turn is hastily drawn. Is it a mountain? A pine tree? A teepee? You see another point in the map, and you turn right at fork in the road. Or is it a river? Or is it a dead tree that is shaped like a Y? The explanations use code words that are puzzling to you.

You suddenly realize that your ancestor was much better at hoarding gold than drawing maps or creating codes because nothing shows you the key information that you need. The confusing, chaotic markings on the map and the odd terminology don't help you. You wish there was a key, some set of rules the person used. Your dreams of gold vanish as quickly as they materialized.

So, what does a coded treasure map have to do with writing a research paper? The research, the books, and quotes and thoughts of others are the treasure (though admittedly not as exciting as gold). If you read a paper or a book that quotes things in some random manner, fails to tell you where the information

◀ Preface ▶

came from, and doesn't have any sort of a bibliography, the paper suddenly goes from being a wealth of useful knowledge that you can use in your own paper to being a useless map that points to nothing.

"MLA" stands for the Modern Language Association, which is the principal American professional association for language and literature scholars. MLA format is generally used by disciplines in the humanities, including composition, literature, philosophy, religious studies, art, and others. The purpose of the MLA is to help organize and strengthen scholarly work and research. One of the ways the association helps the scholarly community is by creating a systematic, rules-based format by which scholars all around the world can construct their papers. This uniformity allows one researcher to pick up the work of another and be able to logically and easily find the materials quoted and referenced.

MLA format, which you will learn in the following chapters, is a way to educate everyone on a system of uniform, rule-based "maps." When you use material from sources, other readers know exactly where it came from and what type of material you have used, so if another student, researcher, or professor reads your work, they can pinpoint exactly where your material was originally found.

This system of rules can be at times confusing since there are so many varieties when it comes to types of sources you can use in a paper. When your professors were in college, they probably only had to worry about quoting from a few types of sources (books, periodicals, government reports, and scholarly dissertations). Now, however, information has exploded. You can quote from these traditional sources, but what about blogs, YouTube videos, websites, and tweets? What about the nature of the modern book, itself? Is it in print from, is it an e-Book from a database your school library gives you access to, is it on a Kindle, or is it a PDF you're reading on your laptop? The staggering options we now face mean that making our treasure map gets increasingly tricky with each new medium with which technology presents us. We hope that our guide can help you de-code what you need to know.

What kinds of classes will require MLA format? Students preparing manuscripts in a variety of disciplines, including the following, use MLA style:

- ◆ English Composition
- ◆ Literature

- Foreign Languages
- Cultural Studies
- Communications

Along with Chicago Style, it is also used in the following disciplines:

- Theater
- Philosophy
- Religion

 BOOK CONTENTS

This book contains seven sections:

Part One: Document Format and Layout

These rules include the details of how to set up your word processor to format the paper you are going to write and submit. It includes where you put the title, how big the margins are, what types of font you should use, where the page numbers go, where your own name and date go, and many other details. The rules are fairly simple, have only a couple of variations, and haven't changed like other parts of MLA format, but they can prove very tricky for students who don't know the ins-and-outs of the software they use. They can also be tricky if you use software that is limited in its functionality, such as Google Docs.

Part Two: Parenthetical Citations

Every time you use material taken from sources in the body of your paper (be it a direct quote or a paraphrase in your own words), you must provide information about the source following the information you use. We do this through in-text parenthetical citations. MLA parenthetical citation rules govern how you create your citations and what goes inside the parentheses. Here, you will start to see variety, depending on the information provided by your sources and the media they are presented in.

Typically, you include the last name and page number in the citation like so: (Vasquez 89). However, what do you do if there is no author, or there is no page number, or there are five authors, or there are numbered paragraphs? These and other variations all matter, so this section of the book covers these rules.

◀ Preface ▶

Part Three: Works Cited Pages

At the end of your paper, you have to provide a list of references for the sources that you used. In MLA style papers, the heading is usually Works Cited. If your sources include lectures, interviews, and other references that are not "works," you will call this list Sources Cited. The entries you must create involve the most rule variations in MLA format, so this is often the most confusing part of assembling a paper. Sources are found in print, online, and in other forms. Plus, if you were doing a paper on a subject like the impact of advertisements on young girls' self-esteem, you'd use data from scholarly journal articles presenting research done on this issue, but you would also have to supply information on the ads that you used as examples—even though you may not think of the ads themselves as "sources" in the traditional sense. If you write about music, films, artworks, etc., you need to supply information in your list of references. Using the proper MLA format for entries is a major challenge since there are so many types of sources. Therefore, this section of the book covers a lot of rule diversity.

Part Four: Writing Logical and Effective Argumentative Papers

Part four contains a new section designed to help you write successful argumentative papers. It gives advice on crafting thesis statements, the types of audience to imagine, appropriate style and language register, the types of sources to draw upon, effective rhetorical strategies, use of direct quotations, structure and organization, and more. One of the key parts to this new section is the addition of an annotated sample student paper that demonstrates how all of these elements come together in a well-written college-level paper. The section ends with a discussion of logical fallacies and how to recognize and avoid them in your own and other people's writing.

Part Five: Understanding and Avoiding Plagiarism

Plagiarism—the theft of other people's words and ideas—can seriously derail a student's grade in a course. Some students, of course, are willing to be dishonest and will deliberately turn in work that isn't their own. However, many students have been charged with plagiarizing sections of their essays and research papers simply because they did not understand when they needed citations or how to successfully summarize and paraphrase passages from works they use as sources. This section covers types of plagiarism, rules for avoiding it, and examples and explanations of improperly and properly paraphrased passages, as well as explaining "common knowledge" exceptions.

Part Six: Brief Guide to Punctuation and Grammar

The Modern Language Association's guidelines follow the same rules of punctuation and grammar that papers in other style formats do. The rules we discuss are by no means unique. But we decided to include this section because many people are uncertain of at least some of the rules that govern sentences. In our experience, many people seem to unconsciously believe in some kind of correct comma-word ratio, and they will sprinkle commas into a sentence that seems longish because they figure there must be some commas in there somewhere—but none may be needed at all. If they have a shorter sentence, they may be worried that they have too many commas even though every single one is necessary. As for semicolons and colons? They seem to baffle almost everybody. We wanted to supply a helpful resources that is as easy to understand as possible. We avoid jargon and focus entirely on the terminology, definitions, and rules that are absolutely necessary to construct grammatical and correctly punctuated sentences.

Part Seven: Practice Exercises and Keys

Part seven contains a series of practice exercises and keys designed to help you perfect MLA format for works cited entries as you prepare yourself for the finished versions of research papers and other types of essays. Few people ever memorize all the variations in MLA format, but even with a manual open in front of you, sometimes following the guidelines can be tricky. The exercises are designed to give you a chance to practice with the format for the types of sources you are most likely to use for college and university papers.

Part Eight: Student Worksheets

Part eight consists of various worksheets that your professor will assign that cover the information presented in the earlier sections. These are varied and include worksheets that can be used as individual homework exercises, in-class work, group work, and quizzes.

PART ONE

DOCUMENT FORMAT AND LAYOUT

 ## Document Layout

Among the first things you'll notice if you ever browse a news website or pick up a newspaper are the headlines of the articles. At the top of every article are several critical pieces of information that you see before you even start to read the piece. These details may seem unimportant, but you learn a lot in the systematic way news sites start their work.

First, you get the title. Without a title, you probably wouldn't bother to read the article at all. The title gives you an idea of what information you are going to find. You will also usually find the author's name and possibly background (such as staff writer or political correspondent). You will also notice a format, the width of the column on the page. These details—the title, the author, the page layout, and the size of the column—are easy for you to read because they are uniform and predictable. If every website you clicked on used a radically different layout, or the next newspaper you picked up listed all the titles on the last page of the paper instead of with the article, you'd be rightfully confused.

The Modern Language Association has developed rules for layout and titles similar to those inherent in journalism, so that all research papers that get written follow a predictable, stable format. This format includes where you put the page number, your name, your professor's name, the date, title, margins, spacing, and any number of other small details.

◀ PART ONE ▶

 General Appearance of Papers

- **Margin Sizes**: Your paper should be printed on one side only with one-inch margins on all sides.

- **Alignment**: Justification is the term for how the type is aligned on your paper. Except for titles and works cited headings, justify the paper at the left margin. Center the title and the heading for the list of works cited in the paper.

- **Font Size**: Choose a simple, legible font like Times New Roman, 12 point. Be sure you use the same font for the entire paper, including block quotations (indented quotations for direct quotations over four lines) and the paper's header.

- **Sentence Spacing**: MLA style recommends using only one space after terminal punctuation marks (periods, question marks, and exclamation points).

- **Line Spacing**: The entire paper should be double-spaced, including your heading; indented quotations (See "Long/Block Quotations" in Part Two); any endnotes, tables, and appendices; and the works cited page. Don't add extra line spaces between paragraphs or above or below titles or in between the works cited entries.

- **Paragraph Spacing**: Indent the first line of each paragraph one-half inch from the left margin, and do not add extra spaces between paragraphs.

- **Fastening**: Simply fasten the pages with a single staple in the upper-left corner. Do not use binders, clips, or folders.

 First Page

Title pages are no longer standard for papers in MLA format. Instead, use a simple personal and class identification heading followed by a title centered above the body of your paper.

◀ DOCUMENT FORMAT AND LAYOUT ▶

Personal and Class Identification Heading

The following information should be in the upper-left corner of your paper; just like the rest of the document, it should be entirely double-spaced. (Do not put this information in the "header" in your word-processing program). This heading comes only on page one of your document.

1. **Your full name.**

2. **Your professor's name.** The title "Professor" should precede the last name; don't use a first name.

3. **The name of the course.** Professors with more than one section of the same class may want students to follow the class name with a colon and the starting time and days abbreviated to the day's first letters, for example, English 1A: 1:00 TR. Online classes can use course reference numbers (CRNs), for example, Art B1: 50121. (These are the only variations in basic document formatting.)

4. **The date the paper is turned in.** The day should precede the month, which should not be abbreviated. See the following example:

Irene Adler

Professor Moriarty

English 1A: 1:00 TR

31 October 2017

Header

The "header" goes in the upper-right corner of each page of your paper and includes your last name and page number. You will want to use the "header" function of your word processor to put it in the correct place in your paper. (In Microsoft Word, choose the "Insert" tab and go to "Header and Footer." From there, choose the "Page Number" menu, and in there, choose "Top of Page.") Your number should be on the upper-right side, plain, with no extra formatting. Precede it with your last name and a single space. Do not include pg. or page, simply the last name and number, such as this: Martinez 8

 ## TITLE

The title of your paper should be carefully thought out and indicate your topic. Avoid titles like "Essay One" or "Research Paper One." Instead, aim for something interesting and informative. Your title should be double-spaced below the heading and centered (remember not to add an extra line—the distance between the last line of your heading and the title should be exactly the same as the distance between each line of the heading and each line of the rest of the paper). Use the center alignment icon in your toolbar to properly center the title; do not simply hit the spacebar until it looks like the title may be centered.

The title should not be followed by a period, but you can end it with a question mark if you can develop an interesting and informative rhetorical question as a title. Don't italicize or underline your title or put it in bold type or within quotation marks. However, if you use part of a work's title within your own title, it should be formatted properly.

The following title contains the title of a short story:

Minimalism in Raymond Carver's "The Bath"

The following title contains the title of a film:

Homer and the Coen Brothers: Greek Myth in *O Brother, Where Art Thou?*

<u>Capitalization of Titles</u>: Capitalize all words in titles except the following (unless they are the first or last words of a title or subtitle): articles ("a," "an," and "the"), prepositions ("of," "with," "above," "in," "over," "before," "at," etc.), coordinating conjunctions ("for," "and," "nor," "but," "or," "yet," "so"), and the "to" in infinitives (as in "How to Capitalize Titles"). You should also capitalize the words that follow hyphens in compound words. If you have a subtitle, use a colon after the title (unless the first part of your title is a question). If your title is lengthy enough to go to two or more lines, create an inverted pyramid shape. Here is an example:

Gender Roles, Films, and Television: The Role of Media in Changing Attitudes in France, Germany, the United Kingdom, and the United States

ITALICS VERSUS QUOTATION MARKS

One of the tricks to mastering MLA format (and writing in general) is learning how to correctly format the titles of different types of sources. You have undoubtedly noticed that some titles are put in quotation marks and others are italicized or even underlined. As a quick and casual rule, "big" sources get italicized, but "little" ones—the ones that are contained inside the bigger ones—are enclosed in quotation marks. This is a generalized guideline, but a good one to remember in most cases. (An exception to the size guideline is a pamphlet—pamphlets are quite small, but they are self-contained.)

If a source is larger, can stand on its own, and may contain other works, put it in italics. If the source fits inside a larger source or "container," enclose it in quotation marks. You might get confused when you look at how some sources, such as newspapers treat titles. They are not using MLA format. Newspapers never italicize text, so they put books, films, periodicals, and other sources that we italicize into quotation marks instead. This does not mean that you should do so in your college papers.

There is one other thing to note—sometimes titles of works contain the titles of other works. If a title that you put inside quotation marks includes the title of something that should be italicized, it is simple: just make sure that works that should be italicized are italicized. If a title that you put inside quotation marks includes the title of something that should also be enclosed within quotation marks, use single quotation marks (the apostrophe key) for the work inside. If a title that you put in italics includes the title of something that should also be italicized, then put the internal title into regular, non-italic font so that it clearly stands out as a title.

Continue onto the next page for a table outlining the differences:

ITALICS VS. QUOTATION MARKS

Italicize the title of the following	Use quotation marks for the following
Book or play (*Understanding Hamlet: A Student Casebook to Issues, Sources, and Historical Documents*; *The True Believer*)	Essay, short story, poem, titled book chapter, titled act from a play ("What We Talk about When We Talk about Love"; "The Raven")
Scholarly journal; these are also referred to as academic journals and peer-reviewed journals. (*Journal of Popular Culture*)	Periodical article ("Confronting Confirmation Bias: Giving Truth a Fighting Chance in the Information Age")
Newspaper (*The New York Times*)	Newspaper article ("Viral Lies")
Magazine (*Time*; *Rolling Stone*)	Magazine article ("Walking Dead Creator Plots American Werewolf in London Remake")
Website (*DoctorsWithoutBorders.org*; *The Huffington Post*)	Posting or article on website ("How To Recognize a Fake News Story")
Feature film or documentary (*Star Wars*; *Food, Inc.*)	The specific scene of a movie, often called "chapters" in the feature of a DVD ("Farewell, Dear Bilbo")
Television series (*Star Trek*; *American Gothic*)	Specific episode of a television show ("The Trouble with Tribbles")
Encyclopedia (*Encyclopedia Britannica*)	An article from an encyclopedia ("Sojourner Truth")
Music album, such as a CD, downloaded album, vinyl record, etc. (*Purple Rain*; *The Downward Spiral*)	Individual song ("Purple Rain"; "Hurt")
Pamphlet (*Know Your Voting Rights*)	
Work of art (painting, sculpture, etc.) (*The Persistence of Memory*)	
Ship, aircraft, or spacecraft, etc. (*RMS Titanic*; *Apollo 13*)	

◀ DOCUMENT FORMAT AND LAYOUT ▶

The Wonderfully Boring History of Italics

Several years ago, MLA format gave us the option of choosing either to italicize or to underline the larger titles listed above. Now, however, they must be italicized. Why in the past would they allow you a choice between the two? It was because people could not create italics when handwriting or typing on standard typewriters. Underlining a title told a publisher or professor that this title was supposed to be italicized. Now, since virtually everyone has access to computers and can italicize the titles that need it, underlining is no longer considered a "synonym" for italics in the work that you formally submit.

You might still have cause to underline titles in your own work. For example, if you are handwriting a draft of an essay or cannot get access to a word processor, or if you are taking note cards in a library using a reserved book that can't be checked out, you should underline text in your notes to remind you of what you need to italicize later on.

Numbers in MLA Papers

Generally, spell out numbers that can be written in a word or two (or three words, as with adjectives describing age: three-year-old twins), for example, ten, twenty-five, and one million. Use numerals for more complicated, lengthy numbers: 3 1/2 instead of three and a half, 1,313 instead of thirteen thousand and thirteen, and so on. Large numbers may be written in a combination of numerals and words, such as 13.3 million. Use numerals for all numbers that precede abbreviations of units of measurement, with other abbreviations and symbols, in dates, in street addresses, in decimal fractions, in numbered series, and in works cited entries and in-text citations. However, if a number starts a sentence, spell out the number or re-word the sentence so that you can use a numeral inside it.

Other Examples:

ten pounds	12 lbs	31 May 2016
thirty percent	95%	315 East 86th Street
five dollars	$5.75	9.5 (This is a decimal fraction)

In ranges of numbers, including those within citations, give all numbers in numeral form in full up through 99. For numbers over 99, only provide the last two digits of the second number unless more are needed for clarity. For example, if the first page of a work begins on page 101 and ends on page 110, 101-10 is clear. If the first page of a work begins on page 1,345 and ends on 1,352, 1,345-52 is clear. However, if the first page begins on 289 and the last page is 301, you should prove both numbers in full: 289-301 If the first page of a work begins on page 1,889 and it ends on page 1,932, drop only the first numeral of the second number: 1,889-932.

 ### Dates in MLA Papers

In the bodies of your papers, do not abbreviate dates. You may use either the day-month-year style or the month-day-year style in the body (remember the identification information in the upper-left corner of the first page must use the day-month-year format). Just be consistent with the style you choose. If you use the month-day-year style, follow the day with a comma. Remember that in works cited entries, we only abbreviate months over four letters long.

Bodies of Papers	**Works Cited**	**First Page, Upper Left Corner**
31 October 2016	31 Oct. 2016	31 October 2016
October 31, 2016		

 ### Potential Problems in Word Processing Programs

MLA paper layout is the part of MLA format that is perhaps the easiest since there are no rule variations. However, many word processors pose challenges to achieving proper MLA format. The most popular word processing software in the world is Microsoft (MS) Word. The default settings of this program cause difficulty for students trying to set their paper up in proper MLA documentation layout.

Extra Line Spacing Between Paragraphs: By default, MS Word adds an extra space between paragraphs, and this extra space makes your document more than the standard double space required in MLA. To change this, go to the Home Tab, and then hit the Paragraph settings. When the dialog box opens, click the box that says something like "Don't add space between paragraphs of

◄ DOCUMENT FORMAT AND LAYOUT ►

the same style." The wording may vary based on your edition of the software. Make sure you do this before you type anything or after you do a "Select All," or the change will only be applied to the line the cursor is on.

Bottom Margins: One of the most frustrating things for writers to adjust is the bottom margin. In spite of your setting the bottom margin to the proper one inch that MLA requires, MS Word often pushes lines of text to the next page, making the printed margin much larger than one inch. There is no simple fix for this other than modifying your margins as you go to make sure that bottom margin comes as close to an inch as possible when the document is printed out. Sometimes getting into the paragraph settings and working with what is called Widow/Orphan controls will help, but not always.

Font Changes: Often students change the font of their paper from the default (which for MS Word is Calibri 11 point) to something professors prefer, such as Times New Roman 12. However, changing the font in the body of the document does not change the text in the header. You may need to access the page's header to change the font there, as well. Remember, you should only use one easy-to-read, standard font throughout the paper.

Spelling and Grammar Checking: Using this feature is important—it not only helps you to catch and correct typos and misspellings, it will prompt you to add missing accent marks where needed (all you have to do is accept the suggested change, which is very handy if you don't know how to add accent marks on your own), it will warn you if you have accidentally typed extra spaces between words, and so on. But you need to remember that programs cannot really think. Sometimes they will flag something as ungrammatical when it isn't. Also, sometimes they will suggest a correction that isn't correct when they come to a misspelling.

If you blindly accept all suggestions, you may be creating startling—and occasionally hilarious—errors. They are hilarious for your professors, that is, who frequently exchange emails within their departments quoting such sentences from students' papers. The errors aren't so funny to the students when it comes to a their grades. Here are a few examples from just one semester:

"Advertisements are immense offenders when it comes to eating disorders and general problems with one's psychosis."

◀ PART ONE ▶

"In and around Kern County, certain areas of the dessert are cultivated by irritation."

"Many male professors may not have the ineptitude to teach an all-male class."

The point is, be careful. Use the dictionary to look up words if you are not sure what they mean. Also, make sure the spell check didn't change a source's or a professor's name to something ridiculous. Remember—programs can't think. You have to.

URLs and Hyperlinks: You may have to copy and paste URLs into your paper, as when you create works cited entries for sources you find online. Word will often make these hyperlinks "live," which will add underlining and change the color. You do not want underlined, paler font URLs when you turn your paper in. Let your cursor hover over the hyperlink, and select "edit hyperlink"; that will give you the option to remove the hyperlink. You may have to do this more than once, as when you "break" the URL to make it fit on the lines in your works cited entries.

Google Docs: Many students struggle with Google Docs once they begin setting up their work in proper MLA format. Though it is a terrific tool for group publication, it lacks the robust formatting options of Microsoft Word, Pages, or the free Open Office or LibreOffice programs. Also, if you are in an online class and your instructor inserts comments electronically throughout your paper, you cannot read them using tools like Google Docs.

PART TWO

PARENTHETICAL CITATIONS

Your favorite band has finally announced its first tour in years, and it is actually coming to your town. Thanks to millions of other fans (and ticket-buying companies and their computerized ticket-bots), you know you've only got mere minutes to score tickets for you and your friends before they are sold out. You are watching the clock in the corner of your laptop, and the instant the clock trips over to 8:00 AM, you click on the link to take you to the ticket-buying website. However, something goes wrong. Instead of a chance to get the best seats, you merely see "404 Error—Page Not Found." The hyperlink that was supposed to land you the tickets is broken, and by the time you go back to the website, the tickets are already sold out. Bummer.

The hyperlink is important in life, and we trust them to work. They take us deeper into the rabbit hole that is the Internet. But when the link doesn't work, it can be a temporary setback, or a massive disappointment (if you didn't get your concert tickets). This is the same basic principle that an MLA parenthetical citation has for a paper. When you read a book or an article for a class, and you hope to use the information in your paper, you rely on citations to be a low-tech equivalent of a hyperlink, guiding you to the source and better, deeper research. When there is no citation, you can't follow the source, and you have a similar sensation (though perhaps much nerdier) to not being able to buy those concert tickets.

So what is a citation? A citation is a systematic process to let readers know where every bit of outside information in your paper comes from. In some books, you will find footnotes at the bottom of the pages, and in others, you will find endnotes at the very end of the book telling you where all the information hails from. In MLA format, however, you use **parenthetical citations**. This means that every time you quote, summarize, paraphrase, or use a date or fact from an outside source, you immediately put information inside of parenthesis at the end of the sentence. The reader uses this information as a primitive hyperlink to find the details of the source later on in the Works Cited page at the end of your paper.

 ## When to Use Parenthetical Citations

MLA papers use in-text citations rather than footnotes or endnotes for publication information. You need to indicate the sources that you use each time you take information from them. In most cases, this means the citation will contain the last name of the author you are referencing and the page number(s) you found the material on.

Example: A basic citation might look something like this: (Schlosser 57). Schlosser is the last name of the author you have just referenced, and 57 is the page number where you found the information.

You must cite all the nonfiction sources used within papers, whether paraphrased, summarized, or directly quoted, unless the material cited is considered "common knowledge." (The fact that the Titanic struck an iceberg is common knowledge, but the name of her captain and the nautical speed she was traveling at when she struck the iceberg are not.) In-text citations are also used in papers discussing literature for any direct quotations from these works of literature.

 ## List of Parenthetical Citation Rules

The following is a numbered list of the rules in this chapter for what needs to be included inside parenthetical citations for different types of source.

1. One Author
2. Two Authors
3. Three or More Authors
4. No Author
5. Page Numbers
6. No Page Numbers Listed
7. Format for Direct Quotations Four Lines or Less
8. Long/Block Quotations

◀ PARENTHETICAL CITATIONS ▶

9. Placement of Parenthetical In-Text Citations
10. Quoted Material, Source Named Before Quotation
11. Comma and Colon Use
12. Quoted Material from an Electronic Source with No Author or Page Number Given
13. Same Source Used More than Once in One Paragraph
14. Quoted Material that Spans Two Pages
15. Corporate Authors, including Government Agencies
16. Paragraph Numbers in Citations
17. In-Text Citations for eBooks
18. Commonly-Studied Works in Multiple Editions
19. Sources Quoting Other Works
20. More than One Work by the Same Author
21. Two or More Authors with the Same Last Name
22. Information from More than One Source
23. Citations for Films, Videos, and Lectures
24. Works in Time-Based Media
25. Translations of Quotations

What Goes Inside Parenthetical Citations?

The information beginning your in-text citations must correspond to the beginning of the entries on your works cited page so that readers can easily locate the full publication for each source that you use in your paper. Typically, this means that the in-text citation will use the author's last name. However, in some instances there is no author or multiple authors or a corporate author. These variations are all discussed in their own sections below.

1. One Author
With one author, simply provide the author's last name and the page number(s) for paginated works. Do not use a comma. For example, (Carter 60). If you indicate the author in your text, you can simply provide the page number: (60).

2. Two Authors
If there are two authors, provide both last names separated by "and." Do not use commas. For example, (Gilbert and Gubar 174-77).

◀ PART TWO ▶

3. THREE OR MORE AUTHORS
Three or More Authors. If there are three or more, you may use the first author's last name followed by the Latin abbreviation "et al." This means, roughly, "and others." Do not use commas. For example, (Frieden et al. 82). If you have supplied all of the authors in the works cited entry, not just the first author and "et al.," use all of the authors' last names in the citation, separated by commas, and setting the last author off with a comma and "and," for example, (Frieden, Lake, and Schultz 82).

4. NO AUTHOR
If no author is provided, you will typically use part of the title in the citation. Format the words you take from the title as formatted in the works cited entry, using quotation marks for articles, essays, short stories, and encyclopedia entries, etc., and italics for books, plays, and websites, etc.

If the title is a single noun phrase, use the entire title, dropping articles ("a," "an," and "the") if they begin the noun phrase. When the title is longer than a single noun phrase, you should use the first noun phrase if it is enough to take your reader to the correct entry in the works cited list. An article titled "Rice's Vampire Novels" consists entirely of a noun phrase (a noun, "novels," preceded by three modifiers) and would not be shortened. An in-text citation would look like this: ("Rice's Vampire Novels" 1). By contrast, "Rice's Novels of Gothic Romance" can be shortened to its initial noun phrase, "Rice's Novels," so an in-text citation would look like this: ("Rice's Novels" 3). Using the first word, "Rice's," would not be enough because another title begins with the same word, which would confuse readers. If the title does not begin with a noun phrase, you may use the first word of the title (not "a," "an," or "the") if it is enough to direct readers to the corresponding works cited entry.

5. PAGE NUMBERS
Follow authors or important title words with page numbers, if provided by the source, with no commas or abbreviations before the numbers. Do not use the abbreviations "p.," "pp.," "pg." or the word "page" before page numbers; simply provide the page number. If you have used the name of the author (or source if there is no author) in your text, you may supply just the page number in the in-text citation. If the material spans two pages, hyphenate the two numbers.

6. NO PAGE NUMBERS LISTED
When a work does not have page numbers, simply use the author's last name or the appropriate part of the title if no author is provided. For sources with

◀ PARENTHETICAL CITATIONS ▶

no page numbers, provide an in-text citation with the author or word from the title even if you have used the name of the source in your text. An in-text citation makes it clear what information you have taken from the source so that you may avoid accusations of plagiarism. The citation is also helpful because it indicates where the information from the source ends if you are paraphrasing or summarizing rather than directly quoting. That way, your readers won't be confused about where the source material ends and your own interpretations or explanations begin.

7. **FORMAT FOR DIRECT QUOTATIONS FOUR LINES OR LESS**
Enclose direct quotations that are four lines or less in your document in quotation marks (use the quotation key, not the apostrophe key, unless you have quoted material inside quoted material). In the case of a standard quote or paraphrased information, your end periods should be placed outside the in-text citations. For Example, one author says, "It is a brilliant tactic if you think about it" (Vakarian 24).

8. **LONG/BLOCK QUOTATIONS**
With direct quotations five lines or longer (in your text, not the original), we use a different format than what we use for shorter quotations.

- Indent twice the typical paragraph indent, which means one inch from the left margin.
- Do not enclose these block quotations in quotation marks.
- Unlike what we do with shorter quotations, periods should precede in-text citations for block quotations.
- Double space as you do the rest of the paper.
- Use the same font and font size as the rest of the paper.
- If a block quotation contains quoted material, use regular quotation marks around that material.
- If an indented quotation contains internal paragraphing, the first line of the quotation should not begin with a paragraph indention even if one is present in the original source.

9. **PLACEMENT OF PARENTHETICAL IN-TEXT CITATIONS**
Place an in-text citation as close to the quoted, paraphrased, or summarized material as possible without disrupting the sentence. If you use one source and the same page number is throughout a paragraph, you may use one citation

at the end of the paragraph rather than a citation at the end of each sentence. This helps your writing seem cleaner. However, if you have added your own thoughts inside the paragraph, you will need multiple citations to distinguish between your source's ideas and your own.

10. Quoted Material, Source Named Before Quotation

You do not need authors' last names in parenthetical in-text citations for works with page numbers when you have named the authors (or the titles of the work if no authors are provided) prior to a quotation, paraphrase, or summary. When you name authors, use their entire names the first time you mention them in a paper. After that, use just their last names without prefixes like "Ms.," "Mr.," or "Dr." Never use an author's first name alone.

Example: Mark Lloyd states, "Communications policy is central to our unique republic. The great advance in statecraft established by the Founding Fathers in the Constitution was the check and balance of conflicting interests within the structure of governance" (74).

11. Comma and Colon Use

There are different ways of introducing quotations, and they require specific punctuation marks. Before direct quotations, use commas after introductory words like "states," "says," "asserts," "argues," "implies," "alleges," "finds," and so on.

However, you should not use commas before quotations if the preceding phrase flows directly into the quotation without pause, as in the example below (the word "that" after "states" is a clue that you should not add a comma).

Example: Mark Lloyd asserts that "Communications policy is central to our unique republic. The great advance in statecraft established by the Founding Fathers in the Constitution was the check and balance of conflicting interests within the structure of governance" (74).

If you choose to introduce a quotation with an entire sentence or independent clause, you should follow it with a colon:

> Mark Lloyd makes the following observation: "Communications policy is central to our unique republic. The great advance in statecraft established by the Founding Fathers in the Constitution was the check and balance of conflicting interests within the structure of governance" (74).

◀ PARENTHETICAL CITATIONS ▶

or

> Mark Lloyd states the following: "Communications policy is central to our unique republic. The great advance in statecraft established by the Founding Fathers in the Constitution was the check and balance of conflicting interests within the structure of governance" (74).

12. QUOTED MATERIAL FROM AN ELECTRONIC SOURCE WITH NO AUTHOR OR PAGE NUMBER GIVEN

When the source you are referencing has no page numbers or author, use the first noun phrase of the title in the citation. If the title does not begin with a noun phrase, use the first important word if it will direct your readers to the correct works cited entry. Remember, you always need a citation, even a brief one. Example:

> The American Academy of Pediatrics advocates a number of changes to make children safe from gun violence. One suggestion is that the federal government "enact stronger gun laws, including an effective assault weapons ban; mandatory background checks on all firearm purchases; and a ban on high-capacity ammunition magazines" ("Firearm-Related Injuries").

Note: The entire title of the source is "Firearm-Related Injuries to Children in the United States."

13. SAME SOURCE USED MORE THAN ONCE IN ONE PARAGRAPH

You may quote the same source more than once in a single paragraph. As long as you do not include any quotations from other sources or any information that you have thought of on your own in between, you can use one parenthetical citation after the last quotation. Separate the different page numbers with commas.

> "Austen's irony is both worldly and unworldly, finding nothing to be surprised at in human immorality, but nothing to be cynically indulged about either." Her irony is subtle and put to the task of defending the cultural and moral status quo. "One should not be misled by Austen's good-natured irony into imagining that she is, in the modern sense of the word, a liberal" (Eagleton 107, 108).

Note that a comma is used between the different page numbers, not a hyphen, because the student writing the paper is taking different quotations from different pages, not presenting a single quotation, summary, or paraphrase that spans the pages.

14. QUOTED MATERIAL THAT SPANS TWO PAGES
If a quote spans more than one page, you must include both pages as indicated below:

> "I wanted to quiz him [Solo] one more time before I decided how involved to get. After learning from Michael that it was common practice to hire workers and not pay them until after they had completed a year, I was feeling a little more uncertain about what to do" (102-03).

Note that in the preceding example, a hyphen is used between the first and last page numbers, not a comma, because the quotations span two pages; you would do the same for individual sections of summarized or paraphrased material that also span more than one page.

15. CORPORATE AUTHORS, INCLUDING GOVERNMENT AGENCIES
For corporate authors in in-text citations, you should abbreviate words that are commonly abbreviated, such as "dept." for "department." However, do not abbreviate these words in the works cited entries. If the corporate author includes the names of administrative units in the corresponding works cited entry, separated by commas, prove all the names in the citation. Here is an example of a cited direct block quotation and the corresponding work cited entry:

> Once a student reaches eighteen years of age or attends a postsecondary institution, he or she becomes an "eligible student," and all rights formerly given to parents under FERPA transfer to the student. The eligible student has the right to have access to his or her education records, the right to seek to have the records amended, the right to have control over the disclosure of personally identifiable information from the records (except in certain circumstances specified in the FERPA regulations, some of which are discussed below), and the right to file a complaint with the Department. (United States, Dept. of Education)

United States, Department of Education. *FERPA General Guidance for Students.* Government Printing Office, 2011.

◀ PARENTHETICAL CITATIONS ▶

16. Paragraph Numbers in Citations
Some sources provide paragraph numbers instead of page numbers, especially online sources. Provide the relevant numbers, preceded by "par." Add a comma after the author's name. If there is no author, use the first important noun phrase of the title (omitting "a," "an," and "the"). If the title does not begin with a noun phrase, use the first word of the title (omitting "a," "an," and "the") if it is enough to direct readers to the corresponding works cited entry. Do not provide paragraph numbers unless your source provides them—do not count them on your own.

> "Fantasy fiction depends on alternative worlds or spaces within our own world that are almost entirely governed by elements of fantasy, such as the Harry Potter series" (Lewis, par. 5).

17. In-Text Citations for eBooks
Most electronic readers (such as a Kindle) include a numbering system that tells users their location in the work. Do not cite this numbering because it may not appear consistently to other users. If the work is divided into consistent numbered sections, such as chapters, the numbers of those sections may be cited, with a label identifying the nature of the number:

> Mark Bauerlein reveals that "Students reaching their senior year in high school have passed through several semesters of social studies and history, but few of them remember the significant events, figures, and texts" (ch. 2).

> "Digital habits have mushroomed, but reading scores for teens remain flat, and measures of scientific, cultural, and civic knowledge linger at abysmal levels" (Bauerlein, ch. 3).

As in the example above, there is a comma in a parenthetical citation after the author's name if the information in the citation begins with an abbreviated word, such as "ch." for "chapter."

18. Commonly-Studied Works in Multiple Editions
Some commonly studied literary works are available in numerous versions; in these cases, you may follow the page number with other information to make it easy for your readers to find the quoted passages in other versions of the

works. For example, Shakespeare's plays come in various editions, but they are identical. The following are lines 3702 through 3705 from Act 5, Scene Three of Shakespeare's *Richard III*. They are on page 426 of the edition the writer references in the essay:

> I shall despair. There is no creature that loves me;
> And if I die, no soul shall pity me:
> Nay, wherefore should they, since that I myself
> Find in myself no pity to myself? (426: 5.3.3702-705)

19. SOURCES QUOTING OTHER WORKS

You will often find a source that quotes people other than the author. In this case, you will introduce the person who stated the material, but the citation must still refer to the author of the source. So, if a source quotes someone else, indicate the quoted person's name in your sentence, and put the source's name inside the citation preceded by the abbreviation for "quoted in." Do not use "qtd. in" if you are quoting your source's own words; use it only when your source is using someone else's words.

> Former Washington Post political reporter Paul Taylor calls the relationship between incumbent broadcasters and incumbent politicians "the most profitable, exclusive, and mutually beneficial relationship in the new Gilded Age of politics" (qtd. in Krishnamurthy 145-46).

20. MORE THAN ONE WORK BY THE SAME AUTHOR

If you are citing more than one work by an individual author, include the first important word or noun phrase of the title of the work you are citing in addition to the author's name and relevant page number(s).

Separate the author's name (if you need it in the citation) and the title with a comma:

> "Those who want to face their responsibilities with a genuine commitment to democracy and freedom—even to decent survival—should recognize the barriers that stand in their way" (Chomsky, *Hegemony or Survival* 5).

> "The concept of 'intellectuals' in the modern sense gained prominence with the 1898 'Manifesto of the Intellectuals' produced by the Drey-

◀ PARENTHETICAL CITATIONS ▶

fusards who, inspired by Emile Zola's open letter of protest to France's president, condemned both the framing of French artillery office Alfred Dreyfus for treason and the subsequent military cover-up" (Chomsky, *Who Rules* 5).

21. Two or More Authors with the Same Last Name

If the document uses sources by different authors with the same last name, include each author's first initial in the in-text citation (use the whole first name if the initials are the same).

> "I am a novelist, trained to use experience for other ends. Why should I tell the story of my life? I do it because my father is dead now, and I always knew I would have to commemorate him. He was a writer and I am a writer; it feels like a duty to describe our case—a literary curiosity which is also just another instance of a father and a son" (M. Martin 3).

22. Information from More Than One Source

If you have information that comes from different sources, indicate them all, separated by semicolons to indicate that the authors represent different, not coauthored, sources. The following is a paraphrase:

> Throughout the history of the folktale, no matter what their respective classes or status, women across the social spectrum shared and modified fairy tales (Smith 172; Warner 316-17).

23. Citations for Films, Videos, and Lectures

As with online and other electronic sources, use an author's name in a citation if one is available or the first noun phrase if one is not. The first the example below is from *Who Killed the Electric Car?* If you have used a director's name as the first word in an entry about a film, that name is what you should use, as in the second example, which is from the same film. If you have taken information from a lecture or speech, use the last name of the lecturer or speaker, as in the third example, which is from a Ted Talk by transgender model Geena Rocero.

> The destruction over a decade ago of thousands of brand new, extremely efficient prototype electric cars suggests that the auto industry's aversion

to change and its reliance on oil have seriously delayed its ability to implement available solutions (*Who Killed*).

The destruction over a decade ago of thousands of brand new, extremely efficient prototype electric cars suggests that the auto industry's aversion to change and its reliance on oil have seriously delayed its ability to implement available solutions (Paine).

"The world makes you something that you're not, but you know inside what you are and that question burns in your heart: how will you become that?" (Rocero).

24. Works in Time-Based Media

In-text citations for quotations from audio and visual recordings should include times or ranges of times, when possible. Separating the numbers with colons, give the hours, minutes, and seconds as displayed in the media player. In the following example, the quotation began three minutes and eleven seconds into an episode of the series *Veronica Mars* titled "Silence of the Lamb."

Veronica Mars said, "I prefer the biker bar by the train station. I get more attention that way. I'm kidding" ("Silence" 00.03:11-14).

25. Translations of Quotations

If you translate all or part of a quotation from another language, provide the translation's source as well as the quotation's source. The translation should follow the quotation. If the quotation and translation are both in the text, place the second one in quotation marks and parentheses or in single quotation marks, not in parentheses. Cite the original first, followed by the translator. Use "my trans." if you translated the quotation. This should precede the page number of the original.

Claudine was known for her "je ne sais quoi" ("indefinable pleasant quality"; Jones 32; Smith 84).

Claudine was known for her "je ne sais quoi" 'indefinable pleasant quality' (Jones 32; Smith 84).

Claudine was known for her "je ne sais quoi" ("indefinable pleasant quality"; my trans.; Smith 84).

PART THREE

WORKS CITED PAGES

When you go to the movie theater and pay hard-earned cash to watch the latest thriller or romance, you probably leave as soon as the closing credits starts to roll. Who needs to learn the name of the second key grip (and what is a key grip anyway…)? Unless it's a movie released by Marvel Comics—known for Easter eggs and hidden scenes—the average person has no interest in watching the long, slow scroll of faceless names.

However, if you were to attend a movie in Los Angeles, you might get a different audience experience. The town is so filled with industry insiders that many people sit because a friend of theirs was a boom microphone operator or a stunt actor in the film. Even more importantly, someone may work in film and really love the way the sound was mixed. She may be sitting in the theater to see the name of the team that was responsible for sound mixing, so she can hire them when she puts together her own film. The credits of a movie are there to let future generations know who did the work behind the scenes and to let the current generation of filmmakers know who they should contact if they are impressed with someone's work.

This is what a Works Cited page does in a paper. Yes, it is the last page, the one that the average reader handily ignores, but it is a vital piece to your work. It explains all the "behind the scenes" players in the document you have just written—the scholars, journalists, and statisticians who backed up every argument you just made. And another scholar sitting in the audience may be very eager to wait until your paper's "end credits" to find out where a particular idea or piece of data actually came from, so he or she can verify its authenticity or use it his or herself.

The Works Cited page is the final page (or pages) of your paper, containing all the information a future reader or researcher will need in order to find the sources you have relied on in your own writing. Every book, article, podcast,

◀ PART THREE ▶

television show, song, advertisement, live lecture, and personal interview you conducted must find a place on your Works Cited page. The information you used earlier in the parenthetical citations line up with the sources, so the reader can always find where your information was originally found.

Additionally, the information in your Works Cited page must be uniform and consistent, so all scholars are able to find each other's sources. This is why there is so much variety in the types of sources and requirements MLA has for Works Cited pages.

Note: You may find yourself using a lecture or interview in your paper. If you do, MLA format requires the heading Sources Cited instead of Works Cited because, technically, a human being is a "source," not a "work."

 TYPES OF WORKS CITED ENTRIES

The following is a numbered list of the elements in this chapter governing the format for the entries that go on the page or pages listing all of the works used in a paper.

 COMMON FEATURES

1. Basic Rules for MLA Works Cited Entries
2. Core Elements Templates
3. Determining Alphabetical Order

 BOOKS AND PLAYS

4. Identifying and Naming Publishers
5. Cities of Publication

 BASIC FORMS FOR BOOKS AND PLAYS

6. Print Versions
7. Book or Play with One Author
8. Book or Play with Two Authors
9. Book or Play with Three or More Authors

◀ WORKS CITED PAGES ▶

10. Book with No Author Given
11. eBook from an Internet Provider, Non-Subscription Service
12. eBook from a Library Subscription Collection
13. Translators
14. Other Common Contributors
15. Multiple Works by the Same Authors
16. Pseudonyms
17. Works by Corporate Authors, including Government Agencies
18. A Single Article, Essay, or Other Work in a Collection or Anthology
19. Multiple Selections from a Collection or Anthology (Cross-References)
20. Introductions, Prefaces, Forewords, and Afterwords
21. Article from a Multi-Volume Reference Set
22. Graphic Novels and Comic Books

Periodicals: Scholarly Journals, Magazines, and Newspaper

BASIC FORMS FOR WORKS FROM PERIODICALS

23. A Scholarly Journal Article in Print
24. A Scholarly Journal Article from an Online Scholarly Journal
25. A Scholarly Journal Article from a Library's Database

MAGAZINES AND NEWSPAPERS

26. A Magazine Article in Print
27. A Newspaper Article in Print
28. A Newspaper Article or Book Review Published Online
29. An Interview in a Newspaper or Magazine Published Online

Websites

30. Article on a Collaborative Project's Website
31. Authorless Article on an Organization's Website
32. Web Project as a Whole
33. Blogs and Blog Comments
34. YouTube and Other Online Videos

FILM, TELEVISION, DVD, AND RADIO

35. Feature Films and Documentaries
36. Television Series, Episodes, and Interviews
37. Episodes in DVD Sets
38. Radio Programs

 OTHER SOURCES

39. Interviews, Lectures, and Other Addresses
40. Advertisements
41. Tweets
42. Songs
43. Slide-Based Presentations
44. Artworks and Objects

1. Basic Rules for MLA Works Cited Pages

- The Works Cited page always begins at the top of a new page; use "page break" to set it off from the body of your paper (it will automatically have your header with your last name and the correct page number in the upper-right corner).

- Put the heading Works Cited, centered, at the top; everything on the page should simply be double spaced, so don't add an extra space under the Works Cited (nothing on the page should be quadruple spaced).

- The first line of each entry should be flush with the left margin. Each line of an entry after the first should be indented one-half inch from the left. You may want to set up a "Hanging Indent" in your word processor instead of manually hitting the tab key to avoid formatting errors.

- Double-space the list of works cited; do not put extra spaces between the entries.

- All entries must go in alphabetical order using individuals' last names (such as authors, editors, or whomever else comes at the beginning of the entry) or by the first words of titles when they begin an entry.

◀ WORKS CITED PAGES ▶

- When there is more than one creator of a work, reverse the first and last names only of the first person at the beginning of an entry, and don't change the order of the contributors.

- Capitalize the first letter of each word in titles except for articles, prepositions, coordinating conjunctions, and the "to" in infinitives (unless any of these is the first or last word of a title or subtitle). Capitalize the words following hyphens in compound words.

- Use quotation marks around the titles of articles, short stories, poems, TV and radio episodes, and other works located in books, periodicals, websites, and so on (unless they are plays or books).

- Italicize titles of books, plays, periodicals, databases, TV and radio series, films, pamphlets, etc.

- When titles of books or plays are parts of the title of a book, do not italicize these; this makes it easier for readers to identify these as distinctive parts of the overall title.

- Works cited entries begin with either authors (or other creators) and titles or the titles, and we normally follow these titles with periods. However, if titles include another punctuation mark at the end as part of the title, such as a quotation mark or exclamation point, use these instead of adding a period.

- If titles have subtitles, you must set the subtitles off with colons unless the part of the title before the subtitle is followed by another punctuation mark, such as a quotation mark or exclamation point. (To determine if a book has a subtitle, look at the title page and publication data; sometimes the spines or covers of books omit subtitles.)

- Abbreviate all months except for May, June, and July; days should come before the months and years in dates, and no commas are used. For works that span two months, hyphenate the months, for example, Sept.-Oct.

- Only a single space follows a period, not two spaces as previously recommended. (This is true for sentences, too, not just works cited entries.)

- Spaces should follow periods and commas after the individual components in entries, such as authors, titles, publishers, etc.; however, spaces do not follow periods inside most abbreviations made of lowercase letters, such as a.m. and p.m. in entries that involve time-based media.

- The date of access is no longer required for works accessed electronically. However, if your instructor requires the date of access, it should be the last item in the entry, preceded by a period and "Accessed" before the date. End the entry, as always, with a period.

- Abbreviations like "n.p." when no page numbers are provided, "n.d." when no dates are provided, and so on, are no longer used.

2. Core Elements Templates

The following is information about the fundamental underpinning of the MLA's new approach to works cited entries: its new "core elements" approach. This new approach adds terms like "containers" and "locations." We are not suggesting that you try to use these templates when you are formatting entries. It might be more confusing than helpful. But it might be useful to understand the MLA's rationale for the changes it has made.

According to its website, "In the new model, the work's publication format is not considered…. The writer creates an entry by consulting the MLA's list of core elements—facts common to most works—which are assembled in a specific order." The punctuation marks we put after elements in a work-cited entry have changed. In the past, for example, periodicals were not followed by punctuation marks, and books were always followed by periods. In the new model, the first two elements in the first (and sometimes only) container, the author (or editors, in the case of edited works that begin with the editors) and the title of the source are followed by periods. Commas follow other elements until the last element, the "location," which is followed by a period.

1. Author [or book or anthology editor].
2. Title of source.
3. Title of container,
4. Other contributors,

◀ WORKS CITED PAGES ▶

5. Version,
6. Number,
7. Publisher,
8. Publication date,
9. Location.

Here are examples of what these elements stand for:

1. Author or Editor	Carter, Angela. Gilbert, Sandra M., and Susan Gubar, editors.
2. Title of Source	"Title of article, short story, etc.," if part of a larger source; Book (if self-contained).
3. Title of Container	*Title of larger source*, such as book, periodical, or website,
4. Other contributors	If applicable, names of others who contributed to the work, such as editor, translator, director, performer, or illustrator,
5. Version	Use if a specific version or edition is required to distinguish the work from others,
6. Number	Volumes and issues, such as volumes and issue numbers for scholarly journals and volumes in book series.
7. Publisher	Publisher, such as book publisher or production company,
8. Publication date	Years of publication for books, days, months, seasons, and years, as provided, for articles in periodicals, and the same, including times of posting when provided, for articles found online,
9. Location	Page number or range of page numbers for paginated sources; for online sources, DOIs or URLs for journal articles and URLs for other online sources, omitting "http://" and not using angle brackets; some instructors may prefer the word "web" to URLs.

"Other contributors" refers to optional listings of people involved with the creation of a work. If their participation is important to your research or paper, include them, preceding each name (or group of people with the same function) with a description of their function. Following are common descriptors:

- adapted by
- directed by
- edited by
- epilogue by
- illustrated by
- introduction by
- narrated by
- performance by

The MLA deals with other information by charting out additional "containers," providing the following template. Note that elements 1 and 2 (the author and title) are not re-inserted in subsequent containers—they are assumed by their placement in the first container. Commas follow all elements until the last element in the container, which is followed by a period.

Container Two
3. Title of container,
4. Other contributors,
5. Version,
6. Number,
7. Publisher,
8. Publication date,
9. Location.

Container Three
3. Title of container,
4. Other contributors,
5. Version,
6. Number,
7. Publisher,
8. Publication date,
9. Location.

Example:

1. Author: Oesterreich, Detlef.
2. Title of source: "Flight into Security: A New Approach and Measure of the Authoritarian Personality."
3. Title of container: *Political Psychology,*
4. Other contributors,
5. Version,

6. Number: vol. 36, no. 2,
7. Publisher,
8. Publication date: Apr. 2005,
9. Location: pp. 275-98.

Container Two
3. Title of container: *Academic Search Premier*,
4. Other contributors,
5. Version,
6. Number,
7. Publisher,
8. Publication date,
9. Location: doi:10.1111/j.1467-9221.2005.00418.x.

Here is what the work cited entry looks like:

Oesterreich, Detlef. "Flight into Security: A New Approach and Measure of the Authoritarian Personality." *Political Psychology*, vol. 36, no. 2, Apr. 2005, pp. 275-98. *Academic Search Premier*, doi:10.1111/j.1467-9221.2005.00418.x.

3. Determining Alphabetical Order

Alphabetize entries by authors' or editors' last names; the first (or only) author or editor of a work should have his or her first and last names reversed (middle initials follow first names). Do not reverse the first and last names of other individuals. Always leave authors' and editors' names in the order that they are given for a work. Order often represents the primary author or editor of a work.

If the list has more than one work by the same people, alphabetize these works using not only last names, but also the first important words of the works' titles (ignore "a," "an," and "the"). Use three hyphens (no spaces between the hyphens) instead of authors' names for every work by them following the first entry, as long as they are exactly the same—don't use the hyphens of a work with another unless both works feature the same authors in the same order. When a paper has works by an individual and by that same person with collaborators, the work by the single individual precedes the others alphabetically.

If no author is given, put the source in alphabetical order using the first important word of the title (ignore "a," "an," and "the," but do not drop them from the title).

For works from alternative media, such as Twitter, ignore special characters like @ and #, and simply use the first letter or letters of the name or pseudonym following a special character.

The following alphabetized list has an authorless fairy tale, a novel by Neil Gaiman, a short story by Gaiman, a children's book by Gaiman and illustrator Brett Helquist, and another authorless fairy tale.

"The Blue Mountains."

Gaiman, Neil. *American Gods*.

---. "The Return of the Thin White Duke."

Gaiman, Neil, and Brett Helquist. *Odd and the Frost Giants*.

"The Wizard King."

 ## Books and Plays

While this first section focuses on books and plays, it covers format issues that are relevant to other sources, as well, such as what to when there are one, two, or three or more authors given, no authors given, translators, multiple works by single authors, pseudonyms, and so on.

4. Identifying and Naming Publishers

You will find the name of the publisher on a book's title page. When providing publishers' names, omit "business" words and their abbreviations, such as Company (Co.), Limited (Ltd.), and Incorporated (Inc.). With University Presses, replace University with U and Press with P, without periods. Don't

◀ WORKS CITED PAGES ▶

separate UP when "University Press" follows the university. For example, "University of California Press" would be "U of California P." Another example would be "Oxford University Press" becoming "Oxford UP." For all other publishers, give the names in full, keeping terms like "Publishers," "Press," "Books," and so on.

Identifying the publisher can be confusing. More than one entity may be listed, but we usually do not give them all. If a parent company is provided with a division, we usually cite only the division. In the following example. Norton Professional Books is the publishing name you should use, not W. W. Norton & Company.

Norton Professional Books

A Division of W. W. Norton & Company

If both an imprint (a "brand name" that some publishers attach to some of their publications) and the company are given, omit the imprint. In the following example, Anthony Bourdain Books, a line of books, is "curated" by Bourdain. It is an imprint of HarperCollins Publishers. You might actually see the imprint over the publisher on the title page, but the wording and design help you distinguish between them. Look for clues like "Publishers," "Books," and "Press" as part of the name to identify the publisher. HarperCollins Publishers is the name you should use in your works cited entry.

Anthony Bourdain Books

HarperCollins Publishers

Sometimes more than one organization is identified, and each is a separate entity, imprints or divisions of the others. In these cases, provide all the names in the order given, with spaces and slashes between the names. Consider the following example from the title page of *The First White House Library: A History and Annotated Catalogue*:

Pennsylvania State University Press

Bibliographical Society of America

National First Ladies' Library

In this example, you would provide the publishers' names this way:

Pennsylvania UP / Bibliographical Society of America / National First Ladies' Library.

5. Cities of Publication

The MLA has dropped the city of publication from most works cited entries. Exceptions are made for books published before 1900 when no publisher is given and for books published in different countries where changes have been made to the original versions. For example, when English author Anthony Burgess's novel *A Clockwork Orange* was purchased by American publishers in 1962, they didn't think American readers would like the final chapter, so they dropped it. Also, J.K. Rowling's American publishers didn't think that American children would be able to figure out British spelling and terminology. Giving the city is important in situations like this because the cities indicate which versions of the works you are using. Provide the city before the publishing company, followed by a comma (not a colon, as in previous versions of MLA format).

Burgess, Anthony. *A Clockwork Orange*. New York, W. W. Norton, 1962.

Rowling, J. K. *Harry Potter and the Order of the Phoenix*. New York, Arthur A. Levine Books, 2003.

Shelley, Mary Wollstonecraft. *Frankenstein; or, The Modern Prometheus*. London, 1818.

BASIC FORMS FOR BOOKS AND PLAYS

6. Print Versions

Author(s). *Title*. Publisher, year of publication.

7. Book or Play with One Author

Carver, Raymond. *Will You Please Be Quiet, Please?* Vintage Contemporaries, 1992.

◀ WORKS CITED PAGES ▶

Note: When a title ends with a question mark or an exclamation point, do not follow it with a period.

Hoffer, Erik. *The True Believer*. 1951. First Perennial Classics, 2002.

Note: If a book or play was published significantly earlier than the copy that you have, you may include the original publication date, followed by a period, after the book's title.

8. Book or Play with Two Authors

Jones, Judy, and William Wilson. *An Incomplete Education*. Ballantine Books, 1987.

9. Book or Play with Three or More Authors

When you have three or more authors, MLA suggests that you provide only the first author's name, followed by "et al." (You will use this author's first name in the in-text citations, also followed by "et al.")

Frieden, Jeffrey, et al. *World Politics: Interests, Interactions, Institutions*. W. W. Norton, 2013.

If you have a reason to include all of the authors' names, you may do so, despite the MLA's current preferences. Options are allowed. You may wish to discuss the background of each author if your instructor asks you to do so. Remember—always ask your professor's preferences with optional elements.

Wysocki, Anne Frances, Johndan Johnson-Eilola, Cynthia Selfe, and Geoffrey Sirc. *Writing New Media: Theory and Applications for Expanding the Teaching of Composition*. Utah State UP, 2004.

10. Book with No Author Given

If no author is provided, begin with title.

Hazards of Primary Care in Aging Populations. J.B. Lippincott, 1978.

◀ PART THREE ▶

11. eBook from an Internet provider, Non-Subscription Service

Author(s). *Title*. Publisher, year of publication. *Provider*, URL (unless your professor prefers you skip this).

Jenkins, Henry. *Convergence Culture: Where Old and New Media Collide.* New York UP, 2006. *ACLS Humanities E-book,* hdl.handlenet/2027/heb05936.0001.001.

or

Jenkins, Henry. *Convergence Culture: Where Old and New Media Collide.* New York UP, 2006. *ACLS Humanities E-book.*

Charles, John C. Abandoning the Black Hero: *Sympathy and Privacy in the Postwar African American White-Life Novel.* Rutgers UP, 2012. *Project Muse,* muse.jhu.edu/book/19214.

or

Charles, John C. *Abandoning the Black Hero: Sympathy and Privacy in the Postwar African American White-Life Novel.* Rutgers UP, 2012. *Project Muse,* web.

12. eBook from a Library Subscription Collection

Author(s). *Title*. Publisher, date. *Provider*, URL.

Fredrickson, George M. *Black Liberation: A Comparative History of Black Ideologies in the United States and South Africa.* Oxford UP, 1996. *eBook Academic Collection,* web.b.ebscohost.com/ehost/detail/detail?vid=3&sid= b48e0ca5-7987-486c-9180-

◀ WORKS CITED PAGES ▶

87cf5682598d% 40sessionmgr 106 &hid=115&bdata=JnNpdGU9ZW

hvc3QtbGl2ZSZzY29wZT1zaXRl#AN= 143953&db =e000 xna.

13. Translators

If the work was originally published in another language, add "Translated by" followed by the translator's or translators' names, a comma, the publisher, a comma, the year, and a period. Note: a comma is added before "and" when separating two names only when authors' or editors' names are the first components of a works cited entry. In the following example, no comma is used to set off the second translator's name.

Ellul, Jacques. *Propaganda: The Formation of Men's Attitudes*. Translated by Konrad Kelle and Jean Lerner, Alfred A. Knopf, 1965.

14. Other Common Contributors

Sources may have other types of contributor. Provide their names the way the example of the translators shows, preceded by the descriptive term, such as "illustrated by," "introduction by," and "edited by."

15. Multiple Works by the Same Authors

When you are using more than one work by the same authors or editors, organize these works alphabetically using the last name of the first author and then the first important word of the title (ignore "a," "an," and "the"). For every entry for these people after the first entry, use three hyphens instead of their names. Only use the three hyphens if the names are exactly the same and in the same order.

Singer, Peter. *Famine, Affluence, and Morality*. Oxford UP, 2015.

---. *The Most Good You Can Do: How Effective Altruism Is Changing Ideas about Living Ethically*. Yale UP, 2016.

---. *The Life You Can Save: How to Do Your Part to End World Poverty*. Random House, 2010.

Singer, Peter, and Jim Mason. *The Ethics of What We Eat: Why Our Food Choices Matter*. Rodale Books, 2007.

16. Pseudonyms

Some authors publish and appear under pseudonyms exclusively. Others publish works or contribute to creative works under both pseudonyms and their real names. If a paper includes works written by an author (or person in another creative role) who uses both a pseudonym and his or her real name, entries may be consolidated under the individual's most well-known name, or you may create entries with a parenthetical reference after the real name, with the real name in parentheses after the pseudonym. In the following examples, one entry is for a novel, and the other entry is for the film performance of the novel's author, who used his real name in the film's credits, not the more famous pseudonym his novels are published under. David Cornwell is le Carré's real name. Note that the "see also" in the parenthetical element after the real name is italicized.

Cornwell, David (*see also* le Carré, John), performer. *The Little Drummer Girl*. Warner Brothers, 1984.

le Carré, John. (Cornwell, David). *The Little Drummer Girl*. Hodder and Stoughton, 1983.

17. Works by Corporate Authors, Including Government Agencies

Corporate authors include associations, institutions, , and other organizations. Omit "the" before the name of any organization in your entries. Begin with the corporate author if it is not also the publisher. Follow with the title in italics. End with the publisher, a comma, and the date of publication.

Institut National d'etudes Demographiques. *Consequences of Rapid Population Growth in Developing Countries*. Routledge, 1 June 1991.

When a work is both written and published by the same organization, begin with the title, not the organization, and list the organization as the publisher, followed by the date of publication.

◀ WORKS CITED PAGES ▶

Human Development Report: 2015. United Nations Development Programme, 14 Dec. 2015. *Publication Manual of the American Psychological Association.* American Psychological Association, 2001.

If a government agency is the author, begin with the name of the government, a comma, and the agency:

California, Department of Developmental Services.

If there are organizational units that the agency is a part of, add these between government and the agency:

United States, Congress, Senate.

United States, Congress, House.

You may shorten the name of the House of Representatives, as there would be no confusion about what it refers to. If your works cited list contains more than one work by the same government, use three hyphens (with no spaces between them) instead of the author after the first entry by that same author:

---, ---, House.

---, ---, Senate.

---, Department of Housing and Urban Development, Office of Healthy Homes and Lead Hazard Control.

For congressional publications, the following are options that you may include: the number and session of Congress, the chamber (either the House of Representatives or the Senate, remembering to omit "the"), and the type and number of the publication, for example, reports, resolutions, bills, and "miscellaneous documents." The sources provided will identify the publication type for you.

United States, Congress, House, Permanent Select Committee on Intelligence. *Intelligence Authorization Act for Fiscal Year 2016.* Government Printing Office, 2015. 114th Congress, 1st session, House Report 2596.

◀ PART THREE ▶

18. A Single Article, Essay, or Other Work in a Collection or Anthology

We usually refer to a book containing multiple works by a single author as a "collection", while the term "anthology" refers to a published collection of works by a variety of people.

> Author(s) of work. "Title of Work." *Title of Anthology*, edited by editors' names, not reversed (give them in the order that they are provided), publisher, year, pp. first page-last page.

> Baker, C. Edwin. "Implications of Rival Visions of Electoral Campaigns." *Mediated Politics:Communication in the Future of Democracy*, edited by W. Lance Bennett and Robert M. Entman, Cambridge UP, 2004, pp. 342-61.

19. Multiple Selections from a Collection or Anthology (Cross-References)

To avoid unnecessary repetition of publishing information, when you have more than one work from an anthology, provide one entry just for the anthology and provide separate cross-references for each of the works that you take from it. The anthology has all the regular components of a book, with the addition of the abbreviation for "editors" after the editors' names.

A typical cross-reference has only four elements: (1) the author of the work, (2) the title, (3) the editors' last names, and (4) the first and last page numbers.

> Author(s) of work. "Title of Work." Editors' last names only, pp. first page-last page.

If the cross-referenced work did not provide an author, you would have only three elements, beginning with the title. If a work was translated, you would add "Translated by" and the translator's name after the title, followed by a comma.

Note: Sometimes anthologies (for example, textbooks for introductory literature courses) contain not just essays, short stories, and poems, but also plays, novellas, and even entire novels. In these cases, these works' titles are italicized, just as they would be if they were published alone.

◀ WORKS CITED PAGES ▶

Editor(s) of anthology, editors. *Title of Anthology*. Publisher, year.

Remember—all works on a works cited page should be in alphabetical order. Don't automatically group cross-references under their anthologies. They will follow them only if alphabetical order determines it. In the Christine Bachillega entry, "Wonder Tale" was enclosed in quotation marks in the title, so we use single quotation marks (the apostrophe key) to denote them, as we enclose the article's entire title in regular quotation marks.

Bachillega, Christine. "Genre and Gender in the Cultural Reproduction of India as 'Wonder Tale.'" Haase, pp. 179-95.

Haase, Donald, editor. *Mediated Politics: Fairy Tales and Feminism: New Approaches*. Wayne State UP, 2004.

Preston, Cathy Lynn. "Disrupting the Boundaries of Genre and Gender: Postmodernism and the Fairy Tale." Haase, pp. 197-212.

20. Introductions, Prefaces, Forewords, and Afterwords

If introductions, prefaces, forewords, epilogues, and afterwords have their own titles, follow these with periods and enclose the titles in quotation marks. Follow with the descriptive word capitalized and a period, but do not enclose that word in italics. If there is no title, simply use the descriptive word.

Moyers, Bill. Foreword. *The Future of Media: Resistance and Reform in the Twentieth Century*, by Robert McChesney, et al. Seven Stories Press, 2005, pp. vii-xxiii.

or

Moyers, Bill. Foreword. *The Future of Media: Resistance and Reform in the Twentieth Century*, by Robert McChesney, Russell Newman, and Ben Scott. Seven Stories Press, 2005, pp. vii-xxiii.

◀ PART THREE ▶

Schlosser, Eric. "Have it Your Way." Epilogue. *Fast Food Nation: The Dark Side of the All-American Meal*, by Eric Schlosser. Mariner Books, 2012, pp. 255-71.

21. Article from a Multi-Volume Reference Set

Pole, Jill. "Chimera." *The Encyclopedia of Fantastical Characters and Creatures*, edited by Lucy Pevensie, vol. 1, Azim Balda UP, 2017, pp. 198-204.

Note: If you are using only one volume of a reference set, specify the number of the volume that you used. (If there is only one volume in the reference work, the entry looks the same except for the omission of a volume)

22. Graphic Novels and Comic Books

A graphic novel stands on its own, so we italicize the title. Begin with the author. Provide the name of the graphic novel in italics. If the illustrator is different from the author and you want to include his or her name in the entry, follow the tile with the illustrator, preceded with "Illustrated by." End the entry with the publisher and the date of publication.

Moore, Alan. *Batman: The Killing Joke*. Illustrated by Brian Bolland, DC Comics, 19 Mar. 2008.

A comic book issue is contained in its series, so we enclose the title of the issue in quotation marks, followed by a period, followed by the series name in italics. If the issue is numbered, we precede the issue number with the abbreviation for number and place it after the series title or, if there is a contributor listed after the series title, after that person's name. Begin the entry with the name of the writer. Follow with the title. Follow with the series, the number, the publisher, and the date. If there is a stand-alone issue, as in the following example, we italicize the title.

Hopeless, Dennis. *Spider-Woman*. Illustrated by Javier Rodriguez. No. 1, Marvel Comics, Nov. 2015.

◀ WORKS CITED PAGES ▶

 PERIODICALS: SCHOLARLY JOURNALS, MAGAZINES, AND NEWSPAPERS

Periodical is the term for collections of articles and other works published at regular intervals.

Scholarly journals are also referred to as academic journals and peer-reviewed journals because for most journals, panels of experts review articles before they are published. A large number of periodicals and articles can be accessed electronically through databases that institutions subscribe to, such as Academic Search Premier, Business Source Elite, and the Psychology and Behavioral Sciences Collection.

Magazines can have useful information, but scholarly journals are preferable. Magazines usually contain secondary or tertiary information when discussing research (readers are getting the information second-hand or third-hand). Some magazines are aimed at particular ideological groups and will be more biased than more neutral periodicals, both in terms of how articles are slanted and the issues they cover.

Newspapers report news on a daily or weekly basis. As with magazines, they provide only secondary or tertiary information when discussing research. Some newspapers are also aimed at particular groups, and their treatment of news stories and what they cover will be more biased than more neutral periodicals.

In databases, different icons are used to distinguish between different types of periodical. Somewhat confusingly, magazines are represented with an icon saying "Periodical" even though all of these are periodicals. Also, something identified as a review can be from any type of periodical; you will have to look at the name of the periodical and look it up to see if it is from a journal, a magazine, or a newspaper. Following are screenshots of the icons:

Scholarly Journal	Magazine	Newspaper	Review (any medium)
Academic Journal	Periodical	News	Review

23. Basic Forms for Works from Periodicals

Author(s). "Title of Article: Complete with Subtitle." *Title of Periodical,*(volume number and issue number for scholarly journals only), day (if provided) month (if provided), season (if provided; don't add a comma after the season) year of publication, pp. first page-last page.

Note that the authors and the title of the work are followed by periods. Commas separate the other elements, and a period ends the entry of the first "container" (there may only be one). If a work is in an issue that spans two months, hyphenate the two months (Jan.-Feb.). When works are not on consecutive pages, provide the first page and a plus sign. Online sources do not always provide page numbers. Sometimes journals have volumes and not issues, and vice versa. Provide what is given.

For electronic versions, the following would be provided after the pages (or year if there are no pages):

Database or provider (if applicable) and DOI or URL for online sources.

URL stands for "uniform resource locator," and DOI stands for "digital object identifier." Use DOIs instead of URLs if they are provided, as with some journals. These will work for readers even if URLs change. DOIs are made up of a series of numbers and occasionally letters. Cite the DOI preceded by "doi," for example, doi.10.1353/pmc.20000.0021. The URL or DOI follows the database when provided or the year if there is no database. Drop "http//" and "https//" in URLs and DOIs, and note that we put the term "DOI" in lower-case letters: "doi."

The MLA Handbook, eighth edition, states that URLs and DOIs can be eliminated from entries if instructors prefer students not to include them. In these cases, entries would end with the provider or terms like "Kindle edition" in order to make it clear that students are not consulting the print versions of these works. It makes sense to provide clarification that the source was found online. In the seventh edition of *The MLA Handbook*, all entries ended with information about where the material came from. (Any work found in paper form would end with "Print," and online entries ended with the word "web" and the date of access. If your professor asks you not to use URLs, ending the entry with "web" makes it clear how the information can be located. Since a comma and the URL would otherwise follow the year, follow the year with a comma and "web," not capitalized. (A term like "Kindle edition" would clearly indicate an electronic source, but some providers may not.) If there is a DOI, use that number instead of the URL because DOIs enable works to be accessed easily, and they are short. Also, while the MLA now suggests that we should no longer end entries for Internet-accessed works with our dates of access, it concedes that the locations and content of online works can be changed, and so, in some cases, your instructors may suggest that your date of access should end the entry for an online source, as was previously recommended. Precede dates with "Accessed," for example, "Accessed 25 May 2018."

 ## Scholarly Journals

24. A Scholarly Journal Article in Print

Author(s). "Title of Article: Subtitle." *Title of Journal*, volume number, issue number, [day, month and season if provided; don't follow with a comma], year of publication, pp. first page-last page.

Remember the following points:

- When a source has more than one author, set the last author's name off with a comma and "and."

- Don't forget that articles and other works in periodicals are enclosed in quotation marks and that the periodicals themselves must be italicized.

- Publishers and database providers do not provide information in MLA format for you. If an ampersand (&) is part of a title, change it to "and."

- "Volume" is abbreviated to "vol."; use the abbreviation for number, "no.," for an issue.

- Drop the first numeral of the final page number for works that are on pages in the same range of a hundred and the first two numbers of pages in the thousands unless more are needed for clarity (1001-32; 1,892-914).

- Do not drop the first letter of the last page number if both are under 100.

- If a work is not on consecutive pages, provide the first page number and a plus sign (5+).

Pelizzon, Penelope, and Nancy M. West. "Multiple Indemnity: Film Noir, James M. Cain, and Adaptations of a Tabloid Case: The Disappearing Death Chamber." *Narrative*, vol. 13, no. 3, Oct. 2005, pp. 211-37.

25. A Scholarly Journal Article from an Online Scholarly Journal

Author(s). "Title of Article: Complete with Subtitle." *Title of Journal*, volume number, issue number, month and season (if provided; don't follow with a comma) year of publication, pp. first page-last-page. *Provider*, DOI or URL (unless your instructor prefers that you not add either and use "web" instead).

The current MLA committee says that URLs and DOIs are optional, though the use of DOIs is preferred. We recommend DOIs, too, since they are both useful and short. It also stipulates that we may add information to entries for clarity. Adding the word "web" can be helpful when a source is found online if nothing else in the entry makes this clear to your readers. The date of access is also optional; end the entry with it if your instructor wants it included or if you suspect information has been altered since the original publication date (some sources provide notes telling readers this). The following examples are for a scholarly journal that publishes online only. Such journal articles are usually not found in library databases.

Magnusson, Gert. "Being a Vampire Sucks: Regarding the Anonymous Vampires in *Buffy the Vampire Slayer*." *Slayage: The Journal of Whedon Studies*, vol. 9, no. 1, Spring 2011, www.whedonstudies.tv/uploads/2/6/2/8/26288593/magnusson_slayage_9.1.pdf.

◀ WORKS CITED PAGES ▶

or

Magnusson, Gert. "Being a Vampire Sucks: Regarding the Anonymous Vampires in *Buffy the Vampire Slayer*." *Slayage: The Journal of Whedon Studies*, vol. 9, no. 1, Spring 2011, web.

Note: Ordinarily, the end of the first "container" for a journal article would be the page numbers; they would be the "location" in the first "container." Since this journal does not use page numbers, the URL is the "location, which is why it follows the year and comma, not a period. MLA format no longer uses abbreviations like "n.p." when page numbers are not provided.

26. A Scholarly Journal Article From a Library's Database

The journals found in college and university subscription databases usually have print counterparts—though the libraries may have only the electronic versions.

Author(s). "Title of Article: Complete with Subtitle." *Title of Journal*, volume number, issue number, month and season (if provided; don't follow with a comma) year of publication, pp. first page-last page. *Database*, DOI or URL. [Some professors may prefer the database followed by the name of the company, not a URL if there is no DOI and the URL is very long. Ask.]

Remember to put databases in italics. The company supplying the database is optional, but adds clarity. Do not italicize it. Current guidelines stress the role of prudent choice when creating entries. Provide enough information for readers to be able to find the sources should they choose to.

For any source with three or more authors, the MLA recommends that you provide only the first author, followed by "et al."

Thomas, Nicole A., et al. "The Lighter Side of Advertising: Investigating Posing and Lighting Biases." *Laterality*, vol. 13, no. 6, Nov. 2008, pp. 504-13. *Academic Search Premier*, doi:10.1080/ 13576500802249538.

If you believe that you are adding clarity and important information by including all the authors, you may do so. This can be useful in papers where you must discuss the expertise of the authors of sources. But check with your professors—find out if they insist on your using "et al."

> Thomas, Nicole A., Jennifer A. Burkitt, Regan E. Patrick, and Lorin J. Elias. "The Lighter Side of Advertising: Investigating Posing and Lighting Biases." *Laterality*, vol. 13, no. 6, Nov. 2008, pp. 504-13. *Academic Search Premier*, doi:10.1080/13576500802249538.

 MAGAZINES AND NEWSPAPERS

You should format the entries for works in magazines and newspapers the same way that you format entries for works in journals, but without volume and issue numbers. Also, newspapers and weekly and biweekly magazines provide days, which should precede the months.

27. A Magazine Article in Print

> Author(s). "Title of Article: Complete with Subtitle." *Title of Magazine*, date (day-month-year format unless there is no day), pp. first page-last-page. (If an article is on only one page, precede it with p. If it is on discontinuous pages, use pp. and follow the first page number with a plus sign.)

> Weinberg, Steven. "Eye in the Present: The Whig History of Science." *The New York Review of Books*, 17 Dec. 2015, pp. 82-84.

28. A Newspaper Article In Print

> Author(s). "Title of Article." Title of newspaper [city added in angle brackets if not in title unless it is a national paper], date (day month year format) pp. first page-last-page. (If an article is on only one page,

◀ WORKS CITED PAGES ▶

precede it with p. If it is on discontinuous pages, use pp. and follow the first page number with a plus sign.)

If a city of publication is not part of the title of a locally published paper, add it in brackets after the name of the paper. You do not need to add cities for nationally published newspapers, such as *The Guardian*.

Bergman, Joe. "Kit-Fox Probe Begins." *The Renegade Rip* [Bakersfield], 3 May 2016, pp. 1+.

Note: The article above began on page 1 and was continued on page 4.

29. A Newspaper Article or Book Review Published Online

These entries are just like those for print entries, but you add the URL (or the word "web" if that is what your instructor prefers) after the date.

Bergman, Joe. "Kit-Fox Probe Begins." *The Renegade Rip* [Bakersfield], 3 May 2016, www.therip.com/top-stories/2016/05/03/kit-fox-probe-begins/ #sthash.tVRJeqDA.dpbs.

or

Bergman, Joe. "Kit-Fox Probe Begins." *The Renegade Rip* [Bakersfield], 3 May 2016, web.

Note: Sometimes the online versions of articles that are also published in print form supply the page numbers of the print versions. If they do, add them. If they don't, do nothing (don't add "n.p.").

Meredith, D. R. Review of *Hitler, Mussolini, and Me*, by Charles Davis. *New York Journal of Books*, 20 May 2016, www.nyjournalofbooks.com/book-review/hitler-mussolini.

or

◀ PART THREE ▶

Meredith, D. R. Review of *Hitler, Mussolini, and Me*, by Charles Davis. *New York Journal of Books*, 20 May 2016, web.

The preceding article is a book review. If a review does not have a title, write "Review of" and give the title of the book, film, play, or CD properly formatted with italics. If the review has a title, follow the author by the title in quotation marks. Follow it with "Review of" and the title of the book, film, play, or CD.

Note: For people's names, have spaces after the periods following initials ("D. R." instead of "D.R.").

30. An Interview in a Newspaper or Magazine Published Online

Begin with the name of the interview subject. Add the writer after the title of the work, preceded by "Interview with" and followed with a comma, the periodical's name, the date (optional, but recommended), and the URL (unless your instructor prefers that you not add URLs). Some interviews are untitled. In these cases, follow the subject's name with "Interview with" and the interviewer. The format will be essentially the same for other online sources, such as news aggregates and YouTube. (See "YouTube and Other Online Videos") for additional information). In the body of your paper, the interviewee's last name goes in the parenthetical citation. The information in parenthetical citations needs to guide your readers to the beginning words of the correct works cited entries.

The standard entry:

Interviewee. "Title." Interview with (name of interviewer), *Periodical*, date, URL.

Jablonski, Nina G. "Always Revealing, Human Skin Is an Anthropologist's Map." Interview with Claudia Dreifus, *New York Times*, 9 Jan. 2007, www.nytimes.com/ 2007/01/09/ science/ 09conv.html?_r=0.

or

◀ WORKS CITED PAGES ▶

Jablonski, Nina G. "Always Revealing, Human Skin Is an Anthropologist's Map." Interview with Claudia Dreifus, *New York Times*, 9 Jan. 2007.

 WEBSITES

Following is the basic format for sources from the Internet. Also, if your instructor wants you to include your date of access (the MLA no longer requires this), it should follow a period and be preceded by the word "Accessed," for example, Accessed 9 Feb. 2017. This differs from the format previously required by MLA rules.

Author(s). "Title of Article: Complete with Subtitle." *Site*, date, DOI or URL (unless your instructor prefers you to omit the DOI or URL and use the word "web").

31. Article on a Collaborative Project's Website

Morton, Ella. "How England's First Feline Show Countered Victorian Snobbery about Cats." *Atlas Obscura*, 13 May 2016, www.atlasobscura.com/articles/how-englands-first-cat-show-countered-victorian-snobbery-about-cats.

or

Morton, Ella. "How England's First Feline Show Countered Victorian Snobbery about Cats." *Atlas Obscura*, 13 May 2016, web.

32. Authorless Article on an Organization's Website

"Philippines: New President Should Break Cycle of Human Rights Violations, Not Compound Them." *Amnesty International*, 10 May 2016, www.amnesty.org/en/latest/news/2016/05/ philippines-new-president-should-break-cycle-of-human-rights-violations/.

or

"Philippines: New President Should Break Cycle of Human Rights Violations, Not Compound Them." *Amnesty International*, 10 May 2016, web.

33. Web Project as a Whole

Many projects on the Web were developed over a span of time. In these cases, cite the entire range of dates provided.

Creator(s) or editor(s), descriptive term. Site. dates provided, URL.

Jokinen, Anniina, editor. *Luminarium*. 1996-2014, www.luminarium.org.

An example of the Luminarium source without a URL is not provided because, in this case, the URL makes it clear that this is a website. It would be ambiguous otherwise, so it is best to include it.

34. Blogs and Blog Comments

Galbreath, Bill. Comment on "Why I Choose to Challenge Climate Change Deniers." *The Huffington Post*, 19 May 2016, 12:19 p.m., www.huffingtonpost.com/bill-nye/why-i-choose-to-challenge-b_10048224.html.

or

Galbreath, Bill. Comment on "Why I Choose to Challenge Climate Change Deniers." *The Huffington Post*, 19 May 2016, 12:19 p.m.

Nye, Bill. "Why I Choose to Challenge Climate Change Deniers." *The Huffington Post*, 5 May 2016, www.huffingtonpost.com/bill-nye/why-i-choose-to-challenge_b_10048224.html.

or

◀ WORKS CITED PAGES ▶

Nye, Bill. "Why I Choose to Challenge Climate Change Deniers." *The Huffington Post*, 5 May 2016, web.

or

Nye, Bill. "Why I Choose to Challenge Climate Change Deniers." *The Huffington Post*, 5 May 2016, web. Accessed 4 July 2016.

35. **YouTube and Other Online Videos**

The MLA advises the use of URLs, but allows instructors to suggest alternatives, such as using the term "web." It would even be logical to simply end the first entry with the year, since *YouTube* clearly identifies the source as being on the web. Also, the MLA prefers that you use "et al." if your source has three or more authors, but you are allowed to use all of their names if your instructor prefers it.

Creator(s) (if provided.) "Title." *Site*, uploaded by (name of up-loader, as given, if given), date, (time if provided), URL.

"Jonathan Pryce: The American Dream." *YouTube*, uploaded by kynnusk, 6 Oct. 2009, www.youtube.com/watch?v=010jO4_Bs9k.

Note: If an upload time is provided, add a.m. or p.m. after the time, as posted.

Henley, Jon, Phil Maynard, James Armstrong, Pascal Wyse, and Mustafa Khalili. "EU Referendum: Brexit for Non-Brits." *The Guardian*, 31 May 2016, 4:02 p.m., www.theguardian.com/global/video /2016/ may/31/ eu-referendum-brexit-for-non-brits-video-explainer.

or

Henley, Jon, et al. "EU Referendum: Brexit for Non-Brits." *The Guardian*, 31 May 2016, 4:02 p.m., web.

Film, Television, DVDs, and Radio

Movies, radio programs, TV series, and episodes of TV series are different from other works in that there are usually no "authors" in the traditional sense. The names we provide in works cited entries for these sources are determined by the importance of their roles in the creation of the works. If we are not focusing on a particular individual's contribution, we begin with the title and follow it with the name of the director and, if desired, other important participants, such as performers and writers. Next, we provide the name of the company, organization, or other group responsible for producing or distributing the work, and then the date. Since more than one group may be involved, we generally cite the one with the greatest responsibility, but that is not always easily determined. In such cases, name them as listed.

36. *Feature Films and Documentaries*

"Feature film" refers to a movie that is a work of fiction, such as *The Martian*, or to a fictionalization of real people and events, such as *Snowden*. The name comes from the fact that most such movies are full-length films intended as main program item in a movie theater. (Film shorts are treated exactly like feature films in entries). "Documentary" refers to movies using pictures, film footage, and interviews with real people involved in real events to provide a factual record. Entries for films differ from other types of entry because how you begin the entry depends on whether you are focusing on the movie in your paper or on specific contributors. The most common entry focuses on the film itself.

Film. Directed by name of director. (Optional: other contributors), Studio/production company, date.

Hot Coffee. Directed by Susan Saladoff, If Not Now Productions, 2011.

You can also begin a film entry with the contributor your paper is focusing on. That format follows:

Name of director(s) or other contributors, role. *Title*. (Optional: other contributors), Studio/Production Company, year.

◀ WORKS CITED PAGES ▶

Washington, Denzel, director and performer. *Fences*. Performances by Denzel Washington, Viola Davis, and Mykelti Williamson, Bron Creative, 2016.

A film may also appear in different versions. Add the version before the company.

Gilliam, Terry, director. *Brazil*. Performance by Jonathan Pryce, director's cut, Embassy International Pictures, 1985.

Gilliam, Terry, director. *Brazil*. Performance by Jonathan Pryce, "Love Conquers All" version, Universal Pictures, 1985.

Note: If both of the Gilliam entries were on the same works cited page, you would use three hyphens instead of Gilliam's name for the second entry. Also, if different versions of films are released in different years, follow the name of the film with the earliest year and end the entry with the year of the version in the entry.

37. Television Series, Individual Episodes, and Interviews

The standard entry:

Series title. Created by (and/or other contribution) contributor(s), company (or companies), beginning and ending dates.

Breaking Bad. Created and produced by Vince Gilligan, performances by Bryan Cranston, Aaron Paul, Anna Gunn, R. J. Mitte, Dean Norris, Bob Odenkirk, and Jonathan Banks, High Bridge Entertainment, Gran Via Productions, and Sony Pictures Television, 2008-2013.

"Gray Matter." *Breaking Bad*. Created and produced by Vince Gilligan, directed by Tricia Brock, written by Patty Lin, High Bridge Entertainment, Gran Via Productions, and Sony Pictures Television, 24 Feb. 2008.

Note: If a paper is focused on a particular contributor, you can begin with that person's name.

Cranston, Bryan, performer. *Breaking Bad*. High Bridge Entertainment, Gran Via Productions, and Sony Pictures Television, 2008-2013.

Gilligan, Vince, creator and producer. *Breaking Bad*. High Bridge Entertainment, Gran Via Productions, and Sony Pictures Television, 2008-2013.

Programs in other "containers":

If you are referencing a series or an episode of a series that you take from another source, that source is part of a second "container." Following the date, which is the "location" and last element in the first "container," supply the added information:

Bosch. Developed by Eric Overmeyer, Amazon, 2015-2016. *Amazon Prime*.

Othello. Directed by Orson Welles, Marceau Films, 1951, uploaded 31 Jan. 2013. *YouTube*, www.youtube.com/watch?v=EmjWIMMtjDc.

"Truth and Advertising." *South Park*. Directed and written by Trey Parker, Comedy Central, 2 Dec. 2015. *Hulu*, www. hulu.com/watch/911398.

For an interview conducted on television, give the name of the person being interviewed, followed by "Interview with" and the name of the interviewer. Follow with the program, the network, and the date. Note that TV networks are not italicized or enclosed in quotation marks.

Goodwin, Doris Kearns. Interview with Trevor Noah. *The Daily Show*. Comedy Central, 29 July 2015.

38. Episodes in DVD Sets

If you are using a disc from the DVD set of a television series, your entry should contain information about the discs, the company that produced the DVD set, and the year of the set's release.

◀ WORKS CITED PAGES ▶

"Episode." *series*, contributors, episode, Company, year, disc number.

"Pilot." *Breaking Bad: The Complete Series*, created by Vince Gilligan, performance by Bryan Cranston, episode 1, Sony Pictures Home Entertainment, 2014, disc 1.

39. Radio Programs

Begin with the name of the segment in quotation marks, followed by "Narrated by" and the narrator, followed by the name of the radio program in italics, followed by the name of the radio network, followed by the broadcast date. Note that radio networks are not italicized or enclosed in quotation marks.

The standard entry:

"Segment Name." Narrated by narrator, *Program*, Network, date.

"Fossils Suggest That Island Life Shrank Our 'Hobbit' Relatives." Narrated by Christopher Joyce, *Morning Edition*, National Public Radio, 8 June 2016.

Many radio programs and segments of their episodes can also be accessed via written transcripts online. Note that even if you are looking at a written transcript, you still need to credit the radio network.

"Fossils Suggest That Island Life Shrank Our 'Hobbit' Relatives." Narrated by Christopher Joyce, *Morning Edition*, National Public Radio, 8 June 2016. Transcript, www.npr.org/sections/thetwo-way/2016/06/08/481263190/fossils-suggest-that-island-life-shrank-our-hobbit-relatives.

Many radio programs feature interviews. Give the name of the person being interviewed, followed by "Interview with" and the name of the interviewer. Follow with the name of the program series in italics, the network (not italicized or enclosed in quotation marks), and the date the interview was first broadcast.

Whedon, Joss. Interview with Terry Gross. *Fresh Air*. National Public Radio, 9 May 2000.

 OTHER SOURCES

40. Interviews, Lectures, and Public Addresses

Sometimes your sources are people you interview or hear in public settings.

When you conduct the interview, you do not need to include your name. Begin with the person being interviewed, followed by "personal interview" and the date. the name of the person being interviewed, followed by "Interview with" and the name of the interviewer. Follow with the city, and the date.

Rice, Becky. Personal interview. 1 Apr. 2017.

For lectures and other public addresses, such as speeches, give the name of the speaker, followed by the title of the lecture or address. Follow with the sponsor of the talk, the date, and the city. If the city is included in the name of the venue, you do not need to repeat it.

Speaker. "Title." Sponsor, date, Venue, City.

Stevens, Jennifer C. "Ideology in the Poetry of Raymond Carver." California Carver Association, 28 May 2010, Hotel Marriott, San Francisco.

41. Advertisements

Begin with the company or other entity that created what is being advertised. Follow with the word "Advertisement" and a period if an ad doesn't have its own title. If it has a title, follow with the magazine, TV or radio network, site, etc., that the advertisement was found in or on in italics followed by the date. Conclude your citation with the page number on which the advertisement appeared if it was in a print medium, followed by a period. Occasionally, magazines with full-page advertisements will not number the page of the advertisement. In such cases, don't make it up yourself. The Dior ad in the magazine Vanity Fair featured below takes up

◀ WORKS CITED PAGES ▶

two pages, front and back. The page number given before these pages is 24, and the page number following is 25. If an ad is found online, end with the URL (as always, drop "http//"). Following are examples of ads found in three different media.

Periodical:

Entity advertising product. "Advertisement's Name" [or the word "Advertisement" if it doesn't have a name; most won't]. *Periodical*, date of publication, page [If provided].

Dior. Advertisement. *Vanity Fair*, Feb. 2017.

EdgeCraft. Advertisement. *The New Yorker*, 30 Jan. 2017, p.69.

Website:

Entity advertising product. "Advertisement's Name" [or the word "Advertisement" if it doesn't have a name]. *Website*, date of posting, URL.

Hyundai. "A Better Super Bowl." *Superbowl-Ads.com*, Feb. 2017, superbowl-ads.com/2017-hyundai-super-bowl-51-li-tv-commercial-better-super-bowl/.

Television:

Entity advertising product. "Advertisement's Name" [or the word "Advertisement" if it doesn't have a name]. Network, date of airing.

Budweiser. "Born the Hard Way." NFL Network, 5 Feb. 2017.

Note that TV networks are not italicized or enclosed in quotation marks.

42. Tweets

While it might have seemed a bizarre idea just a few years ago to think that a quotation disseminated though tweeting would ever be quoted in a research paper, that situation has now changed. We can think of any number of reasons, such as a student writing a paper that mentions current political discourse, why tweets would be quoted. Begin with the tweeter's @name, then, using quotation marks, quote the entire tweet with original capitalization and punctuation. Follow with the site, the date and time posted, and the URL. When you are organizing the entry alphabetically, the @ is ignored. In the example we give, the person twittering uses his real name. If someone does not use something clearly identifiable, but you know the name, it should be enclosed in parentheses without reversing the first and last names after the @name and followed by a period after the closing parentheses.

@name (first and last name if needed). "Quotation exactly as given." *Site*, date, time, URL.

@stephenfry. "Oh no my husband has found an even more attractive older man! Eek." *Twitter*, 26 Feb 2017, 10.28 p.m., twitter.com/stephenfry/status/836105761910464512.

43. Songs

How songs are treated in works cited entries depends on the medium of release and whether a song is part of a collection or is released on its own, not as part of a larger work, like an album. If released on its own, the title of the song is followed by the recording label or other publishing entity and the date of release.

Song from an album:

Artist(s). "Song Title." *Album*, recording label, date of release.

Cohen, Leonard. "Sisters of Mercy." *Songs of Leonard Cohen*, Columbia, 1967.

If you find a song online, follow the date with a comma and the URL (as always, drop "http//").

◀ WORKS CITED PAGES ▶

44. Slide-Based Presentations

Generally, if someone uses PowerPoint (or a similar type of slide presentation, such as Apple's Keynote), that is simply going to be part of a lecture or speech, and there is no need to have a specific works cited entry other than the one for the lecture or speech. But sometimes students find slide presentations online and want to use them in papers. While the MLA has not provided examples, the following format logically fits within its guidelines. Since a presentation like this is stand-alone, it should be italicized, no matter how short it is.

Author(s). *Title*. Medium, uploaded (provide date, time, etc. as given), *Site*, URL.

Jennings, Jamie. "The Case of the Many Faces of Cinderella." PowerPoint, uploaded Summer 2002, *Pete's PowerPoint Station*, fairytales.pppst.com/cinderella.html.

45. Artworks and Objects

Begin with the creator, who may be a painter, sculptor, photographer, architect, designer, etc. Follow with the title in italics. If there is no title, use a generic description, capitalizing the first word. Do not put the description in italics. Follow with the date of creation, the name of the museum or other place of presentation, and the city it is in. You do not need to repeat the city's name if it is part of the name of the work's location.

Creator(s). *Title* [or description]. Creation Date, location, city.

Bourgeois, Louise. *The Nest*. 1994, San Francisco Museum of Modern Art.

Mapplethorpe, Robert. Polaroid photograph. 1972, Whitney Museum, New York.

Naso, Albert J. *Home in the Woods*. 2000, private collection, Bakersfield, California.

Tiffany, Louis Comfort. Table lamp. 1905, M. H. de Young Memorial Museum, San Francisco.

PART FOUR

WRITING LOGICAL AND EFFECTIVE ARGUMENTATIVE PAPERS

Here is a common occurrence: you have finally "unlocked" the MLA "code," you have done all of your research, and you are ready to write an A paper that astounds and entertains your professor, friends, and fellow students. You've finally figured out how to use your word processor to set your margins, add your header and title, double space everything, and make sure that your works cited entries are properly indented. You know how to draft a perfect Works Cited page, and your in-text parenthetical citation skills are on point. However, as you stare at the document on your screen, blank except for your personal and class identification information, header, and title, all that white space is overwhelming, and the blinking cursor looks like it is hungry.

Don't worry. We've got you covered. This chapter looks not at the technical MLA format issues involved in writing a paper, but at how to generate rock-solid content effectively presented in a well-organized structure. Despite the importance of a paper's MLA documentation, content is key. What will you say? How will you say it? When do you need to bring in your expert sources, and how much detailed information from them do you need? What kind of audience should you be imagining? What should your style be? If you have questions about how to generate a strong thesis statement, structure a paper, determine the type of evidence you need, choose type of appeals to make, and how to avoid logical fallacies and errors in reasoning, read on.

 TYPES OF PAPERS

The three most common types of paper are expository, analytical, and argumentative. All three of them are important to college-level writing, but they are different types of college paper. Each has its place, depending on the class and the assignment, but some do include and require more critical thought than others.

An **expository** paper is designed to explain or describe something. It provides information, but it does not try to persuade readers to adopt a point of view or take an action. It is basically just an information paper. An **analytical** paper focuses on examination and interpretation in order to analyze something, such as a literary work, historical or cultural event, or a work of art. It is more sophisticated than a simply expository paper. It may even involve making an argument, but the argument is not the main purpose of the paper. It will, of course, involve the careful presenting of relevant information, so it is also informative, but it goes beyond that. The purpose of an **argumentative** paper is generally defined as being to persuade readers to believe that a theory, opinion, or assertion of policy or action is superior to other alternatives. Thus, it also has to be informative and analytical, but it is the most sophisticated—and demanding—of the three types of paper. Regardless of which type of paper you are writing, your instructor (and the very nature of the paper itself) will require you to generate a strong thesis statement. Typically, the argumentative paper is the most important paper required in a first year composition course, and it is very often also a research paper. Argumentative research papers are a staple of many subsequent courses, including upper division and graduate work.

 THESIS STATEMENTS

As noted, research papers in composition classes usually must do more than simply present information—they must make and defend arguments. They require debatable thesis statements, not simply assertions of fact. The thesis must be something that reasonable people could have different opinions about. You cannot get away with simply stating an obvious piece of information. Most instructors want a paper that explores a problem and argues in favor of a potential solution—or at least a partial solution. Do you have to think of a solution to a problem that society is facing on your own? Of course not. Instructors of classes focusing on research want you to do *research*—they want you to find out what experts in specific areas have to assert about issues and what evidence these experts can offer. Evidence should be empirical, or at least empirically based; it should depend on research that produces actual data that can be analyzed.

◀ WRITING LOGICAL AND EFFECTIVE ▶

Just remember the following guidelines when crafting a thesis statement for an argumentative paper. A thesis statement should be the following:

1. an **assertion**, not a question;
2. **one sentence long**;
3. **debatable**—this means that you are asserting a position that reasonable people can either agree or disagree with; and
4. **specific**—for example, if your paper is focusing on a problem, it could lead to a discussion of possible solutions.

Regarding the last point, you should ask yourself this question: "What do I want my imagined readers to do?" Think in practical terms. Don't make a suggestion that you cannot picture yourself carrying out. Your thesis should do more than express wishful thinking about what individuals, businesses, industries, professions, or segments of the government "should" do. Look at what professional organizations, consumer advocates, nongovernmental organizations (NGOs,) and governmental agencies, for example, advocate in the way of specific solutions. Look at what experts have proposed. Remember—you are writing a research paper. It's all about presenting the best research possible.

 DEBATABLE THESIS STATEMENTS

Sometimes students have trouble distinguishing between debatable and non-debatable thesis statements, and they create thesis statements that merely state facts.

Example of a non-debatable thesis statement:

> Eating huge quantities of fast food is bad for children's health.

This is not debatable by reasonable people. A person would have to be pretty unreasonable to advocate eating huge quantities of any kind of food, let alone fast food, which is known to be unhealthy.

Example of a debatable thesis statement:

> The United States should ban fast food marketing in both print and electronic media aimed at children under the age of thirteen.

This is an example of a debatable thesis because reasonable people could disagree with it. For example, some people might think that any restrictions aimed at limiting fast food advertisements to children would amount to a violation of corporations' First Amendment rights. Other people might disagree with them, pointing out that we already have laws designed to protect children regarding advertisements for alcohol and tobacco products. These are not the only two stands that people can take, but they are examples of ways that reasonable people can have different opinions.

By the way, if you are going to argue in favor of legislation, you need to know the steps that people take. A fun and useful resource is the video "I'm Just a Bill," which first aired on an educational series called *Schoolhouse Rock* back in 1973. According to CNN, more than 30 million people have since watched the *Schoolhouse Rock* videos on YouTube, and "I'm Just a Bill" is one of the most popular. It describes how a bill can become a law by passing both houses of Congress and then going to the White House, where the president must sign it. There are other resources, but this is a fast and fun introduction. You should not simply state that "the government" should make something happen—discuss what ordinary people like you and your readers can do to help get laws passed.

 NARROWING THESIS STATEMENTS

Generally speaking, the narrower—that is to say, the more specific—your thesis is, the more effective your argument will be. You have to support your thesis statement with evidence, and that is easier to do when you limit it to something very specific.

Example of a thesis that is too broad:

> The United States should ban cruelty against the animals used for food production.

There are several reasons why this statement is too broad and too vague. What does "cruelty" mean? We know what words like this mean to us, but other people may have widely differing ideas on what is too cruel to be tolerated. Even "food production" may be too vague—does this include only animals raised to actually be food, or does it also involve animals used for producing eggs, cheese, and milk?

◀ WRITING LOGICAL AND EFFECTIVE ▶

Example of a narrower thesis:

> The Humane Slaughter Act of 1978 requires the humane handling of animals slaughtered in USDA inspected-slaughter plants except for chickens and other birds; it should be expanded to apply to all animals, including birds.

While agreeing on the definition of "humane handling" may seem to pose a problem, the thesis refers to a specific law, which actually does establish legal definitions, and these can be supplied in the body of the paper.

This thesis could even be reduced to the following, as long as the introductory sentences leading up to it supply the necessary information:

> The Humane Slaughter Act should be expanded to require the humane handling of all animals, including chickens and other birds, which are currently exempted.

Think of the thesis statement you generate as tentative. While you need to have a thesis in mind as you do your research, you should be prepared to refine it or even make major changes to it as you learn more about the topic.

As you plan your argument paper, you need to decide what approach you should take in support of your tentative thesis. You have to decide which types of "appeals" to employ.

Ethos, *Logos*, and *Pathos*

Over 2,000 years ago, the philosopher Aristotle taught that there were three essential types of appeal a speaker could use to sway an audience: *Ethos*, *Logos*, and *Pathos*. Today, these three appeals are as important in writing as they are in public speeches.

Ethos refers to a writer's or speaker's character as perceived by the audience. An *Ethos*-based argument stresses how you present yourself. Audiences are usually more likely to accept the arguments of people they see as honest, sensible, and knowledgeable. *Ethos* is conveyed by a writer's style, such as word choice and the types of arguments employed. Be careful to be conscious of your audience and your writing purpose.

When you look at your own arguments to consider your use of *Ethos*, ask yourself these questions:

1. What audience should I picture?
2. How do I want my audience to picture me?
3. What register (the degree of formality conveyed by word and sentence structure) is most appropriate for my writing situation?
4. What tone (apparent attitude toward the subject) is most appropriate?

As noted earlier, you should picture a diverse audience, not just people who are like you or who already agree with you. You probably want them to see you as logical, reasonable, honest, and fair. You can best do this by showing that you are capable of understanding all sides of an argument and by avoiding informal fallacies, especially ones like "arguments against the person" (attacking people instead of dealing with the merits of their arguments) and "straw person" (misrepresenting other people's arguments instead of dealing with the real ones). You also want them to see you as a person who has become something of an authority on the subject that you are discussing.

You can help achieve this by introducing genuine authorities to your readers and establishing their credentials. Be alert to the tone your writing has; you don't want to look too casual or sound sarcastic. The tone that would work in a message to a friend is probably too informal for a research paper. Also, humor can work in some situations, but it can also be risky. Jokes can fall flat. Punctuation and grammar are important, too. If your sentences are awkward or obviously ungrammatical, you look less credible.

Word choice should also be a consideration in how you present yourself as a writer and thinker. Don't fall into the trap of trying to use "big words" that you normally aren't comfortable with. You should certainly try to develop your vocabulary so that you are able to choose the most accurate and precise words, but a thesaurus or dictionary won't tell you how words will strike your audience or how they fit best into sentences. Instead of making you look smarter, the "big word" strategy can backfire, sometimes comically—only the joke is on

◀ WRITING LOGICAL AND EFFECTIVE ▶

you. Instead, enhance the credibility of your image by the evidence you can produce and the way you handle it.

1. When you read other people's arguments, you should consider their use of *Ethos*. To do so, you should ask the following questions:
2. What assumptions does the writer make about the audience?
3. What methods does he or she use to bolster the appearance of credibility?
4. What does the writer's language say about him or her?
5. What does the writer's tone convey?
6. Does the writer claim any connection, whether direct or ideological, to well-known people in order to seem more impressive? If so, how credible is the connection?

Logos means both "word" and "reason." This type of appeal is based on logic. A *Logos*-based argument stresses rational thought. In everyday situations, our arguments often depend on *Ethos* and *Pathos*, but academic arguments require an emphasis on *Logos*. This does not mean that you should not be conscious of your image or that you should always refrain from trying to touch your audience's emotions; you just need to present factual evidence and logical chains of reasoning to support all of your claims.

Recognizing the types of arguments that are employed, as well as proper identification of premises and conclusions and the logical connections between them, are crucial aspects of logos-based writing. Some arguments are based on definitions, such as what certain terms mean or what the true nature of something is. Some arguments employ analogies or draw parallels between different situations. Many arguments assert cause and effect relationships. Some depend on facts and expert opinions.

When you look at your own arguments to examine your use of *Logos*, ask yourself the following questions:

1. Are all of my premises clear?
2. Are they sound or are they simply assumptions or prejudices?
3. If any of my premises are implicit (unspoken), would they work better if I made them explicit (clearly stated)?
4. Do my premises clearly support my conclusions?

5. Is my language clear and precise?
6. Have I defined all important terms that my audience might not understand?
7. Are any analogies or parallels I have used really strong? (Do the relevant similarities outweigh the dissimilarities?)
8. Have I drawn on genuine experts and accurately represented their ideas? Have I provided their credentials?
9. Have I provided empirical data and statistics?
10. Have I avoided formal and informal fallacies? (There will be more on these later in the chapter.)

As a participant in the scholarly community, you want to do everything you can to make your arguments stand up to careful scrutiny. This sometimes means being willing to rethink and even abandon some of your original assumptions. Indeed, that type of hard consideration is often the core of true critical thinking.

When you read other people's arguments to consider their use of *Logos*, you should ask the following questions:

1. Are all their premises clear, and are they sound, or are they simply assumptions, prejudices, or generalizations?
2. Are there any missing premises?
3. Is the language clear and precise? Do any important terms need clarification, and are any important terms used inaccurately?
4. If any analogies or parallels have been used, do the relevant similarities outweigh the dissimilarities?
5. Does the writer draw on genuine experts, and are their credentials provided?
6. Can you find sources to check to see if their ideas are presented accurately? What facts and statistics have been provided, and can they be verified?
7. Are there any formal or informal fallacies?

Pathos is appeal based on emotion. A *Pathos*-based argument stresses how you can summon feelings in others. Use of emotion isn't in itself always a bad thing. In fact, there are many issues that should engage our emotions. We simply need to be careful not to let emotions get in the way of rational thought. We can find many examples of the use of *Pathos* in arguments in everyday life.

◀ WRITING LOGICAL AND EFFECTIVE ▶

Advertisements appeal to many of our emotional needs, such as the desire to be attractive and popular or the fear of aging or death. Politicians appeal to emotions as diverse as fear, anger, self-interest, patriotism, and love of family. Emotional appeals may also hinge on people's images of themselves. Most people want to think of themselves as fair, compassionate, and intelligent, and appeals that bolster the audience's self-image can also be quite effective.

Different emotional appeals can be used for different outcomes, not all of them logically legitimate. For example, often arguments that stress people's fears appeal to prejudices and misinformation. Arguments designed to rouse an audience's anger are also often connected to prejudices and misinformation. Making an audience laugh at someone can encourage them to dismiss that person's ideas even when they are legitimate (the "argument against the person" fallacy). Aristotle warned his audience 2,000 years ago that playing on people's emotions in order to manipulate them and cause them to ignore logic and evidence corrupts judgment and harms both individuals and society.

When you look at your own arguments to examine your use of *Pathos*, ask yourself the following questions:

1. Am I emphasizing emotion rather than empirical evidence? If so, how can I fix this?
2. Do I risk alienating readers by presenting my arguments in such a way that I implicitly or explicitly belittle the opinions of people who might disagree with me? If so, how can I fix this?
3. Do I seem to be taking for granted that most readers probably feel the way that I do, and am I letting that make me believe that I have a stronger argument than I really present? If so, how can I fix this?

When you read other people's arguments to consider their use of *Pathos*, you should ask the following questions:

1. How do I feel about this issue? Is it one that I have trouble being open-minded about?
2. If my emotions seem to be the same as the writer's, have I allowed this to make me overlook any flaws in the arguments presented?
3. Is this writer trying to rouse any emotions in the audience? If so, what are they?

4. Does the issue itself tend to raise emotions? How do these emotions differ in different groups of people?

Recognizing how *Ethos,* *Logos,* and *Pathos* may all play a part in arguments can help us, no matter what type of argument model we use or what we find in the texts that we read. If you consider these three types of appeal and how they are represented in the works you read while doing research and in your own writing, you'll be one large step closer to mastering information literacy and writing strong, persuasive argumentative papers.

 AUDIENCE

Always keep your imagined audience in mind. Don't imagine only your instructor or classmates; imagine the general public, which is composed of a wide variety of people. Don't assume that your audience is familiar with all of your examples or sources. When writing about a source, do not assume that everyone has read it. Ask yourself what your readers will need to know to understand the points that you are making. When we write something, we know what we mean to say. Therefore, it seems clear to us when we read it over—after all, we've just digested our own source material. But the people we should be imagining haven't read everything that we have. Define concepts the first that time you mention them. In some instances, a definition may be particularly important because there may not be one agreed upon definition. In these cases, you should acknowledge the lack of a widely agreed upon definition, discuss how definitions differ, and stipulate the definition that you will be using in your paper.

Keep in mind that a significant part of the general audience that you should imagine as you write would be composed of people who are skeptical about what you are trying to prove to them. Imagine different political, social, and cultural viewpoints. Even if you are picturing a fairly specific audience, like parents, students, members of your own community, or some other group, you should think of a diverse group of people within that population.

Don't assume that all your readers are just like you. Avoid value judgments and terms and phrases like "moral," "immoral," "right," "wrong," and so on. These do not have the same definitions for everyone. You may believe that anyone

◀ WRITING LOGICAL AND EFFECTIVE ▶

who disagrees with you is wrong, but to write that way is ineffective with a diverse audience.

Adopt a serious, relatively formal, scholarly tone appropriate for your imagined audience. Most instructors want you to avoid informal language, such as slang, vernacular, and idiomatic language. Avoid words like "nowadays," "moms," "dads," "kids," and "stuff." Don't refer to authors by their first names. Avoid first person singular ("I," "me," etc.) and second person ("you," "your") in most academic papers.

 STRUCTURE AND ORGANIZATION

Introductory paragraph. Introductory paragraphs are like "mini-outlines" for your papers, letting readers know what the scope of your paper is and why your topic is important. Try to engage your readers' interest. You might include a direct quotation if it has a strong impact. You can provide background information. Move from the general to the particular, narrowing your focus to your thesis. Introductions don't have to be long—you don't want to ramble or lose a sense of focus—but you are unlikely to interest your readers with only three or four sentences.

In a college paper, the strongest position for your thesis statement, which advances your main argument (major assertion), is at the end of your introductory paragraph—what you want your paper to prove will be clearer to your readers and have a greater impact. Outside of college writing, theses can be anywhere in a work. They can even be implied rather than explicitly stated. For college papers, however, the approach is different. Your paper is evaluated by how well you support your thesis, so it needs to be stated clearly and be easily identified.

Even though we use the term introductory paragraph, in a longer piece of writing, you may end up using several paragraphs in order to establish all of your basic ideas; even still, you will place the thesis at the end of the introduction.

Avoid dull, formulaic phrases like "This essay will prove . . . ," "This paper will be about . . . ," "We will be examining," or "I will discuss . . . ." Such phrases are boring, and they sound stuffy and amateurish. Also, as noted earlier, you should avoid first person singular in most academic papers.

First body paragraph. This is a good place to provide more extensive background information than what you provided in the introduction. It can lay the foundation for what you will provide in the paper in support of your main argument. It can include definitions of key terms and concepts and overviews of key theories. It can help flesh out your introduction.

Supporting evidence paragraphs. The rest of your paper should be composed of distinct paragraphs that present evidence, ideas, and arguments in support of the major argument made in your thesis statement. When you are editing the first draft, ask yourself what point each paragraph makes in support of your arguments. Each body paragraph should contain a topic sentence that tells readers its controlling idea. What is one fact, detail, or example that you should tell your imagined audience that will help them better understand your ideas? The answer would be the topic sentence for a paragraph. A topic sentence can begin a paragraph or be somewhere else in the body of the paragraph.

Read each paragraph you write carefully. If you cannot find a topic sentence, or if you cannot see how the information in your paragraph supports a relevant point, then your readers will not be able to tell, either. It is useful to print out a hard copy of your paper and annotate it. Read the paper as if someone else wrote it. Use a highlighter to identify each paragraph's topic sentence. Write in the margins of the paper, noting how each paragraph offers support to main points.

Make sure to provide clear and logical transitions between body paragraphs. Your paper should not give the reader the impression of hopping abruptly between different ideas. At the close of each paragraph, your reader should have a clear idea of why that paragraph was important to your paper and how it supports your thesis. You can often use the last sentence in a paragraph to provide the transition to the next paragraph

Provide enough detail so that your audience can evaluate the research you cite. You should not expect readers to simply take your word that research means what you say it means or that it means what someone else writing about it or presenting it says it means. Offer significant details that can be evaluated. Don't simply say, "Studies show that [a claim]. . . ." or "Statistics indicate [a claim] . . . ." or "Findings suggest [a claim] . . . ." and leave it at that.

◀ WRITING LOGICAL AND EFFECTIVE ▶

Journalism students are often taught to ask six questions about the subject they are writing about: *Who? What? Where? When? Why?* and *How?* These are useful questions to ask when reading your paper draft and any references you make to research. Reading about the research studies that you refer to, would your readers be able to answer *Who? What? Where? When? Why?* and *How?* If not, you need to include more information. *Who* conducted the research? *What* were the sample populations (size, age groups, etc.)? *What* were the actual results? *When* was the research conducted? *Why* was it conducted? *How* were the data gathered and evaluated?

Don't offer unsubstantiated generalizations and assumptions as evidence. For example, statements like "Americans believe too much fake news" or "Americans spend too much time playing video games and too little time reading" aren't precise, and they don't offer statistics or proof. "Americans" implies all Americans, and "too much" is a vague generalization; it does not provide statistics or data. All of your arguments should be based on assertions that you can back up with empirical evidence.

Introduce expert sources to your audience in the bodies of your papers. Your readers need to know why the sources you choose are credible. Some instructors may ask you to introduce sources by naming the titles of their books or articles. Other may tell you not to do this because that type of information is found on your list of works cited, and it does not explain why people whose information you are using are reputable authorities. They may prefer that you give relevant background information, like credentials, degrees, and specialties for scientists. If an expert is associated with an organization of some kind, you should explain what it is. If an expert is a professor or a doctor, you need to indicate what discipline he or she is a professor or a doctor of.

Introduce experts when you first use their ideas. Use their entire names the first time that you mention them, and use their last names throughout the rest of the paper, without prefixes like Dr., Ms., Miss, Mrs., and Mr. Don't refer to authors using only their first names. Use their first and last names the first time you use them in your paper and just their last names after that.

You do not need to introduce ordinary journalists (reporters) to your audience. They are not experts in the field—they are simply reporting information for newspapers, magazines, and other media. Just cite their last name in an in-text citation. If reporters refer to research studies, don't stop there. Find the studies themselves. It is unlikely that the reporters will provide enough information for readers to evaluate the actual original research.

Counterargument paragraphs. The purpose of these paragraphs is to anticipate your readers' objections and to make your paper more objective and reasonable. Ask yourself what possible arguments your readers could pose against your assertions. Provide one or more of these arguments and then offer logical reasoning and evidence to refute them. Be sure to end a counterargument paragraph with a concluding sentence that reasserts your own ideas so that you do not confuse readers. Soemtimes students alternate stands in every other paragraph, thinking they are providing arguments and counterarguments, when all they are really doing is confusing their audience by making it look like they don't know what they believe.

A counterargument paragraph can follow a supporting evidence paragraph, which can be followed by another supporting evidence paragraph offering new ideas, with a continuing pattern of support, counterargument, support, counterargument. Alternatively, you could follow all the supporting evidence paragraphs with one or more counterargument paragraphs—you may have more supporting evidence paragraphs than counterarguments. The subject and content of the paper will determine this. Sometimes two or more supporting evidence paragraphs may be supporting the same main points, with one providing examples, one providing explanations, and so on. The wonderful thing about writing in the age of computers is that you can tinker with the structure. You may decide that one really long paragraph should be broken down in order to make your points clearer.

Concluding paragraph. Your conclusion should provide a sense of closure to your paper, highlighting the key points that you have made in support of your thesis. A conclusion is not simply a last body paragraph. In many ways, it mirrors the introduction. In an introduction, you tell readers what you will prove and the information that you will cover. In your conclusion, you remind readers of what you proved and why the issues matter. However, your conclusion should not simply restate your introduction. If your conclusion seems to be mainly repetition, it will bore your audience. You should also avoid beginning this paragraph with obvious and redundant phrases like "in conclusion."

◀ WRITING LOGICAL AND EFFECTIVE ▶

Don't add new information into your conclusion. If you come up with new ideas, integrate them into the body of your paper. However, you may add a powerful new quotation if it serves to effectively support your main ideas.

Basic Paper Guidelines

These guidelines are designed to help you to write successful college-level papers. You should review these guidelines before and after you finish the drafts of essays and research papers. Some instructors take slightly different approaches to some areas, such as the maximum allowed percentage of direct quotations in a paper or whether it is acceptable to introduce a source by naming the title of a book or an article instead of discussing the authors' credentials, experience, and expertise, but most of the guidelines reflect standard approaches to academic writing.

Section One: Thesis Statements

1. **A thesis statement is a single declarative sentence that asserts what your essay will prove.** It cannot be a question. It isn't two or three or four sentences; if you find yourself generating more than one sentence, all but one of those should be saved for when you write your paper's introductory paragraph; they can be used to build up to your thesis sentence.

2. **The thesis statements for analytical and argumentative essays should assert debatable points, not just state facts or "factoids."** A fact is something that has really occurred or is actually the case. A "factoid" is an invented pseudo-fact believed to be true because it "feels" true and appears in print, is heard in media, or is simply repeated often.

3. **Unless specifically instructed to do so, avoid thesis statements that express personal value judgments or take moral stands. Argumentative papers should emphasize researchable information.** Remember—your task is not to convince people who already agree with you—you need to convince people who may be highly skeptical.

Section Two: Audience

1. **As noted earlier, always keep your imagined audience in mind. Don't imagine only your instructor or classmates; unless otherwise instructed, imagine the general public.** Always ask yourself what your audience needs to know to understand your evidence and arguments. Don't leave out crucial information.

2. **Avoid exclusionary language, like "man," "manmade," "chairman," and so on.** This type of language is no longer considered acceptable, according to MLA and other academic and journalistic standards. Use terms like "people," "humanity," "artificial," and "chairperson." Try to be sensitive about terminology when referring to groups of people.

3. **Adopt a tone and register appropriate to your assignment.** You will be writing many different kinds of papers in college, and you may be encouraged to be personal and informal in some assignments. However, for most classes that require argumentative papers, your tone should be fairly formal. Also, find out what your instructor thinks about using first person singular and second person pronouns.

Section Three: Sources, Evidence, and Support

1. **Choose scholarly sources for essays and research papers. Look for the research, data, and theories of experts in a given field.** Scholarly journal articles and books by experts in the fields that you are looking at are the best sources. Scholarly journals are also referred to as "academic journals," "refereed journals," and "peer-reviewed journals." The terms "peer-reviewed" and "refereed" mean that a panel of peers in a particular field has read the articles submitted to a journal in that field and have decided that they are supported by careful research. Journals are superior to magazines because magazines' primary purpose is making money, and the contents are not aimed at scholars. Also, some magazines are biased in particular directions. For information from books, read book reviews in reputable sources to see how respected the research contained in them is.

◀ WRITING LOGICAL AND EFFECTIVE ▶

2. **Investigate the sponsors and purposes of organizations and websites. They may not always be what they purport to be.** If you go to a site's "About" page, and it indicates that another group sponsors it, look that group up. Keep going until you reach the end of the chain. It may take you back to a corporation or a group with a political agenda.

3. **As suggested earlier in this chapter, provide enough detail so that your readers can understand and draw their own conclusions about the research and evidence that you discuss.** Don't forget to introduce expert sources to your readers in your paper, just saying that they are experts without providing information about their research isn't enough. Sometimes students drop quotations into their papers from authorities and leave it at that, assuming that quoting an authority is enough to bolster their arguments. The quotations themselves may just be generalizations—we need to know why an authority believes what he or she believes—how were those conclusions reached? What proof was offered?

4. **Don't include evidence or ideas that you do not fully understand.** You may find yourself undercutting or contradicting your own ideas without even realizing it. Do not use terminology unless you are absolutely sure of what the words mean, either in your own sentences or when you directly quote. If you do not understand all of a source's words or ideas, don't use them.

5. **Unless otherwise instructed, avoid referring to yourself and your feelings and experiences.** Never forget your imagined audience—a group of diverse people interested in the issues that you are examining, not in you, personally.

SECTION FOUR: PROPER ATTRIBUTION OF IDEAS

While the following points are covered in greater detail in other sections of the book, we icnlude them here as a reminder to look at with the other guidelines before you submit the final drafts of your papers.

◀ PART FOUR ▶

1. **All papers must have works-cited pages, and all sources in your papers must be included.** Review the proper format for works-cited entries, and remember that entries begin with the authors or, in the case of works with no authors given, the full titles of the works.

2. **Papers must properly attribute information to the sources you use with in-text citations. When you take information from sources, use in-text citations even when you do not directly quote. ALL information you take from sources in your paper must be followed by in-text citations.** Not properly attributing information is a form of plagiarism, which can result in a failing grade.

   When you have sources with pagination and have mentioned the authors in the body of the essay, all you need in the citations are the page numbers. If you have not clearly indicated the source in your essay, you will need the last names of the authors or, in the case of a work with no author given, the first important noun phrase of the title before the page number.

   For sources without page numbers, always use in-text citations even when you have indicated the source of the information in the body. These citations will clearly indicate exactly what you are citing. Thus, even if you use the author's name to introduce a quotation, summary, or paraphrase, include it in parentheses at the end of the information you take from the source. This will also make clear where the information that you have taken from the source ends.

3. **Do not copy phrases or sentences from sources without enclosing them in quotation marks or, in the case of direct quotations over four lines, omitting the quotation marks and indenting the quotations one inch from the left margin.** Not indicating when you use someone else's exact wording is a form of plagiarism, and plagiarized papers can earn failing grades. Having an in-text citation after the information is necessary, but not enough.

4. **Paraphrase and summarize using your own words. Just changing a word or phrase here and there is not an acceptable paraphrase.**

◀ WRITING LOGICAL AND EFFECTIVE ▶

As noted earlier, give your sources credit for their ideas even when you put them into your own words.

5. **Do not use your sources' in-text citations.** You should tell your readers where your sources got their information if they discuss other people's research, but presenting their in-text citations implies that you read the original research when you did not. You should explain the research and name the researchers and identify their expertise. See if you can access their articles through the library's databases and legitimately cite them directly.

6. **Punctuate your citations properly. Periods follow in-text citations if you do not have indented quotations.** Do not end the sentence preceding the citation with an extra period—the period that follows the citation is sufficient. If what precedes the in-text citation is a direct quotation, you will have the quotation mark, a space, the parenthetical citation, and the period.

7. **Quotations that exceed four lines in your paper should be indented one inch (usually two default tabs) from the left margin, and the quotation marks should be omitted.** With indented quotations, the period precedes the in-text citation.

8. **Use "qtd. in" inside in-text citations if your source quotes someone else.** For instance, Thurgood Marshall wrote, "In recognizing the humanity of our fellow beings, we pay ourselves the highest tribute" (qtd. in Greenway 58). Only use "qtd. in" (the abbreviation for "quoted in") when your source is quoting someone else, not when you are quoting the source, and make sure that you clearly indicate in the body of your work the name of the person, organization, or other source being quoted.

9. **Only use paragraph numbers in citations for sources that count the paragraphs for you.** Do not try counting paragraphs yourself—those numbers would not appear when your readers go to the source you used, so these numbers would not be very useful, and it is easy to make mistakes.

Section Five: Use of Quotations

1. **Make sure that your quotations connect logically to what you have just been writing.** Do not add quotations that have only a vague connection to what you have been talking about only because you are supposed to have a certain number of sources. Make sure that they provide evidence for a point that you have made, not just vague generalizations. As you edit your paper, every time you see a quotation, ask yourself these questions: "What important point am I illustrating with this?" "How does this connect to the topic of this paragraph?" "What would people who have not read all of the information that I have read as I studied my topic need to know to better understand this?"

2. **In most cases you will need to explain and elaborate on quoted material to help your audience understand it. Don't assume that quotations can stand alone.** Give them context—ask yourself what added information you would need to understand the quoted material if you were reading it in someone else's work. Remember that quotations are there to support your points, and you need to clarify them and make connections for your readers. Your chosen quotations may seem clear to you, but that is because you have read the work that you are quoting from.

3. **Avoid having back-to-back quotations.** Having two (or more) quotations in a row with no comments or connections is ineffective. You need to add context and clarifications between quotations. Connect the quotations to the purpose you believe they can help serve in your paper.

4. **Check with your instructor, but a general rule of thumb is that no more than 20% of a paper should be composed of direct quotations.** There is no limit to the amount of paraphrased or summarized information that you provide—you need to present your research. Just don't forget to cite *everything*. And remember that paraphrasing involves more than changing a word or two here and there.

◀ WRITING LOGICAL AND EFFECTIVE ▶

5. **The word "quote" means to use someone else's exact words; it does not mean "states."** Thus, for example, if you quoted an author named Maria Tatar from an article about her childhood, you would write that Maria Tatar states, "I grew up in the shadow of the Holocaust. In the 1950s, a lot of things like the diary of Anne Frank were appearing, and reports of the Nazi atrocities were coming out in the newspapers," not Maria Tatar *quotes*, "I grew up in the shadow of the Holocaust. . . ." *You* are quoting Tatar—in this passage, Tatar is not quoting anyone; these are her own words.

 SECTION SIX: EDITING AND PROOFREADING

1. **Editing means looking at how information and ideas are presented.** With editing, the focus is on content and clarity. Editing involves implementing changes to make a paper better organized, better argued, more suited to the imagined audience, and more easily understood. Editing is as crucial a part of writing as getting your ideas down the first time. It should occur multiple times throughout the writing process, but it is especially important before you turn your paper in.

2. **Proofreading means finding and correcting typographical errors and mistakes in punctuation, grammar, style, and spelling.** Reading your papers out loud can be helpful (as can having a friend read it out loud to you while you follow along with a print copy). Reading papers backward, sentence-by-sentence, is also helpful because it breaks your flow of thought, and you are more likely to see what you really wrote instead of what you meant to write.

3. **Finish a first draft of your paper at least two or three days before it is due. It is virtually impossible for most writers to catch all of a paper's problems after it has just been written.** You need to put a paper aside for a little while before you can read it as if another person wrote it—that is, with a truly critical eye. You are more likely to see where you need further evidence or clarifications. You may realize that some information in the paper should be presented in a

different order than what you started with. Also, when we have just written something, our brains helpfully fill in details or skip over problems—our brains know what we *meant* to say, but they don't always tell us what we *did* say. We can easily miss mistakes that are obvious to other readers and that would be to us, too, if we had looked at our work again even twenty-four hours later.

4. **Print your paper and work with a hard copy when proofreading and editing.** Try to read the paper as if someone else wrote it. Use a highlighter in one color to identify each paragraph's topic sentence. Use a highlighter in a different color to identify sentences that you think need further explanations or evidence. Use a pen or pencil to fix typos, punctuation and grammar errors, and to rewrite sentences or phrases. Don't be afraid to cross phrases, whole sentences, and even whole paragraphs out—it is easy to get repetitious without even noticing. A crucial part of editing is learning what to throw out as well as what to build upon.

5. **Use the spelling and grammar checking tools in your word processing program.** You make a very poor impression when an instructor reads a paper and glaring spelling errors are scattered throughout it. It makes it look like you didn't take the assignment very seriously or that you just didn't give yourself enough time to do a proper job. These tools can catch more than spelling and grammar errors. For example, they let you know if you are missing an accent mark and can provide it. Sometimes we have too many spaces between words or are missing spaces between words. These tools will alert us to these problems, too. Just remember that software can't think. That is why reviewing grammar rules helps. The software may identify something as ungrammatical that isn't.

6. **Make sure that you use the appropriate software functions when formatting your document.** Your header must be inserted using the "header" function, your title must be centered using "center," your works cited page must be set off using "page break," and so on.

7. **It is also helpful to have friends, family, or tutors read your papers**—get as many readers as possible—and ask them to be honest.

◀ WRITING LOGICAL AND EFFECTIVE ▶

Tell them not to worry about hurting your feelings—they will be doing you a favor if they are bluntly honest. *Everyone's* work can be improved.

8. **When your final draft is finished, ask yourself if you have an interesting and informative title** to draw your audience in, not something like "Essay One" or "Research Paper." Try to think of a title that makes your topic clear and that might interest your imagined audience.

 TYPICAL COLLEGE PAPER GRADING RUBRIC

A grading rubric is a scoring tool used by teachers to explicitly represent the performance expectations for a paper or other assignment. A grading rubric provides clear descriptions of the characteristics of an assignment associated with each level of level of mastery. Your professor may use the following rubric or one very much like it. At the top you see a description of an A paper, followed by papers with decreasing levels of mastery. Use this rubric to remind yourself of what you should strive to achieve—and what you should strive to avoid.

A Level: You did what the assignment asked for at a high level of quality, demonstrating thoroughness, critical thinking, and skilled use of sources. You demonstrated an understanding of the material and the ability to generate an argumentative thesis statement and to defend it logically and with sufficient, even superior, evidence. Work in this range is complete in content, well organized, and shows that you took extra steps beyond what was explicitly required. The paper is almost entirely free of typos and punctuation, grammatical, mechanical, and format errors, and you used the correct word processing tools, such as "page break" and "header." Your sentences show a clear purpose. You vary your sentence structure in order to craft rhythmic prose and keep your audience interested. You are not required to revise, but you may be a perfectionist who can't stop yourself.

B Level: You did what the assignment asked of you at a proficient level, generally demonstrating thoroughness, critical thinking, and competent use of sources. Work in this range is mostly complete in content and well organized. You demonstrated a basic understanding of the material and the ability to generate an argumentative thesis statement and to defend it logically and with evidence, though there may be room for improvement in both areas. You may need to review the assignment's instructions and paper guidelines a little more carefully. It may have some typos and punctuation, grammatical, mechanical, or format errors, but not enough to be distracting. You used the correct word processing tools, such as "page break" and "header." Your sentence construction may be mostly correct, but it may lack imagination, purpose, and sophisticated subordination and coordination. With revision, you could bring your grade up to an A.

C Level: You did what the assignment asked of you at a competent level. Work in this range requires significant revision, but it is largely complete in content, and the organization is logical. You demonstrated an understanding of the material and the ability to generate a thesis statement and to defend it logically and with evidence, but the thesis may have leaned more to the merely informative than to the argumentative. More evidence to support the thesis may be needed. You probably need to re-read the paper instructions and guidelines more carefully. The style is straightforward but unremarkable. It may have noticeable typos and punctuation, grammatical, mechanical, or format errors, but not enough to indicate complete indifference or a lack of understanding of such issues. You may have failed to use the correct word processing tools, such as "page break" and "header." With significant revision, you could bring your grade up to a B or even, with hard enough work and significant improvement, an A.

D Level: You did what the assignment asked of you at a poor quality level, and you may have failed to meet certain requirements, such as sufficient benefits from or types of source or the minimum word count. Work in this range needs significant revision. The content is often incomplete and the organization is hard to discern. You may have failed to demonstrate a basic understanding of all the sources that you used, and you may have failed to generate an argumentative thesis statement or any thesis at all. If you had a thesis, you may not have produced enough evidence to adequately support it. Your paper gives the impression that you did not read the instructions and the paper guidelines very carefully. Attention to style, punctuation, grammar, mechanics, format, and proofreading is often nonexistent or chaotic. You may have shown a poor understanding of competent paraphrasing. You may have neglected to cite some sources at some points.

◀ WRITING LOGICAL AND EFFECTIVE ▶

F Level: You neglected much, most, or all of what the assignment asked of you. You failed to meet a significant number of basic requirements, such as sufficient numbers or types of source, the minimum word count, and/or the correct topic for the assignment. Work in this range often goes beyond needing significant revision—in some cases, the student has failed to meet so many requirements that he or she needs to start over from scratch. You may have failed to demonstrate a basic understanding of the sources that you used, and you may have failed to generate an argumentative thesis statement or any thesis at all. If you had a thesis, you may not have produced enough evidence to adequately support it. Your paper gives the impression that you did not read the instructions and the guidelines carefully enough (or at all). Attention to style, punctuation, grammar, mechanics, format and proofreading may be nonexistent, as is understanding of basic word processing functions. The paper may also have earned a grade of F for plagiarism if you copied sentences or phrases without indicating that these were direct quotations or if you did not cite all sources used.

For the following section, please pay attention to the notations or [Note …] as you read the sample annotated sample student paper. You will find the corresponding annotation in the footnotes on the same page. We encourage you to read these notes as you go through the paper.

PART FOUR

 ANNOTATED SAMPLE STUDENT PAPER

Irene Adler [**Note 1**]

Professor Moriarty

English 1A: 1:00 MW

19 November 2017

The Tragedy of Modern Slavery [Note 2]

Harriet Tubman once wrote, "I think slavery is the next thing to hell. If a person would send another into bondage, he would, it appears to me, be bad enough to send him into hell if he could." [**Note 3**] Tubman would know; she was a slave in the American South who escaped in 1849 and who became both a rescuer of other slaves and a leading abolitionist ("Harriet Tubman"). [**Note 4**]

Note 1: The information in the upper left corner of the first page includes the student's name; the professor's title and last name; the class, its starting times, and the days that it meets; and the date in the day-month-year format. Like the rest of the paper, this information is double-spaced. Use the "header" function to add your last name and the page number to the upper right corner of every page.

Note 2: Titles of students' papers should not be underlined, italicized, in bold font, or enclosed in quotation marks. An interesting title catches the audience's attention There are no extra spaces above or below titles. Nothing in a paper should be quadruple spaced.

Note 3: Opening the paper with a quotation helps to "hook" the reader and generate interest in the subject matter.

Note 4: When an article does not provide an author, use the first important noun phrase of the title in the citation. (Sometimes that will be the whole title.) The title will begin the works cited entry. The source was an article, so it is enclosed in quotation marks. Periods follow in-text citations unless you have an indented direct quotation. Make sure to cite all information in a

◀ WRITING LOGICAL AND EFFECTIVE ▶

Many Americans would be shocked today to learn that slavery isn't a thing of America's past. It is a terrible violation of human rights, causing unimaginable suffering to both children and adults, that is still happening today. [**Note 5**] According to Anti-Slavery International, the world's oldest international human rights organization, "Modern slavery is inflicted on millions of people all over the world. But often it's not called slavery, and many people don't even know it exists" ("What Is Modern Slavery?"). [**Note 6**] The International Labor Organization (ILO), [**Note 7**] which is a specialized agency of the United Nations that deals with labor issues, social protections, and work opportunities, stated in 2016 that "an estimated 40.3 million people are in modern slavery, including 24.9 in forced labor and 15.4 million in forced marriage"; 60,000 of these enslaved people are in the United States. Modern slavery comes in many forms, including sex trafficking, child marriage, domestic slavery, debt bondage, and forced labor ("Forced Labour"). Slavery, which many Americans associate only with the era before the Civil War, is still a huge problem. What can ordinary citizens do about it? [**Note 8**] We can encourage education on the topic, donate to national and international anti-slavery organizations, and

---

paper, whether directly quoted, summarized, or paraphrased. The information following the direct quotation is also from the same source, so only the one in-text citation is needed here.

Note 5: This appeal to *Pathos* is designed to arouse compassionate readers' pity for the victims the writer will be describing.

Note 6: Notice how the introduction starts with broad statements that gradually build up support for the paper's thesis by getting more and more specific.

Note 7: Acronyms follow the terms they stand for and are enclosed in parentheses. After this, a writer can simply use the acronym (in parentheses).

Note 8: A rhetorical question can be an effective introduction to a thesis statement.

learn how to recognize the signs that indicate when people we encounter in our own country are held in slavery. [**Note 9**]

[**Note 10**] Human trafficking is now the fastest growing crime in the modern world. The U.S. State Department is legally required to submit a report each year to the Congress on foreign government efforts to eliminate human trafficking. [**Note 11**] The report uses the term "trafficking in persons," which is used in U.S. law and around the world term to categorize modern-day slavery in all of its forms. According to the 2017 report, "Human trafficking is one of the most tragic human rights issues of our time. It splinters families, distorts global markets, undermines the rule of law, and spurs other transnational criminal activity. It threatens public safety and national security" ("Trafficking in Persons Report 2017" i). [**Note 12**] The report focuses on the impact of slavery on the victims and their families, but, as the preceding quotation asserts,

---

Note 9: The best place for a thesis is at the end of the introduction, where it has the most impact. This thesis clearly indicates what the paper will be about and what solutions the writer will discuss to help solve the problem. Also, it offers an appeal to *Ethos*. The writer presents herself as a person who is concerned about a worldwide problem and who believes that she and other people should involve themselves in the solution.

Note 10: Body paragraphs should have clear topic sentences. They don't have to be at the beginning of a paragraph, but that is often a very good place for them. Also, we do not add extra spaces between paragraphs; we simply indent the first line of a new paragraph one half inch.

Note 11: Always keep an imagined audience in mind of people who have not done the research that you have done. Tell them about the organizations that you name and use as sources of information.

Note 12: Sometimes introductions to reports, books, and other sources use Roman numerals, not Arabic numerals, to number pages. Note that in these instances, the Roman numerals are not upper case.

it also grimly notes that the ramifications of modern slavery have far-reaching effects that can indirectly have an impact on almost everyone. The Department's report describes "the face of modern slavery," noting the many forms that it takes: adult sex trafficking, child sex trafficking, debt bondage, forced labor, domestic servitude, domestic child labor, and the unlawful recruitment of child soldiers (17). [**Note 13**]

Sex trafficking involves women and girls who are forced into prostitution, which is often the result of kidnapping, debt, deception, and fraud. [**Note 14**] Some sex traffickers lure girls from impoverished countries with promises of jobs in more prosperous ones. Then they are beaten, raped and told they must repay their travel expenses by becoming prostitutes. ("Trafficking in Persons Report 2017" 10). Sometimes desperate women initially consent to becoming prostitutes, so many people blame them for their own plight. However, [**Note 15**] "[e]ven if an adult initially consents to participate in prostitution it is irrelevant: if an adult, after consenting, is subsequently held in service through psychological manipulation or physical force, he or she is a trafficking victim" ("Trafficking in Persons Report 2017" 17). Consent is consent only if a person has the right to revoke it.

Note 13: It is best not to end paragraphs with quotations or to allow quotations to stand on their own. Connect them to your topic. Also, the page number alone is sufficient in the citation since the source was already identified.

Note 14: As noted earlier, body paragraphs should have clear topic sentences, which, when at the beginning of a paragraph, should also serve as transitions from the previous paragraph. This sentence makes the transition by naming one of the forms of slavery listed in the concluding sentence of the preceding, paragraph.

Note 15: Use square brackets if you make a change to a direct quotation. Since the quotation was introduced with the writer' transitional term "However," she changed "Even" to "even."

◀ PART FOUR ▶

In the United States, as elsewhere, sex trafficking frequently involves kidnapping. A sixteen-year-old girl was kidnapped in Florida after she accepted an invitation to spend the night with a new "friend" she met at school. [**Note 16**] 16 It turned out that her new friend was actually a prostitute, and her so-called "dad" was a sex trafficker. The sixteen year old was raped and drugged and was being taken to another city to be delivered to a man who had paid $300,000 for her when she was rescued by her family with the help of an anti-trafficking group (Celizic). [**Note 17**]

Sex trafficking not only includes women and or girls being forced into prostitution, but also domestic workers who are forced to be the sexual slaves of their employers. These domestic workers are usually children ranging in age from five to eighteen years old. [**Note 18**] They are for the most part girls, but boys can also be victims ("Trafficking in Persons Report 2017" 17). Poverty and tradition play a big part in how these children become domestic slaves. In some parts of the world, sending their children to work in a wealthy family is seen as an opportunity for them to continue school and learn domestic skills. The children are isolated from their families and become dependent on their employer, which enables the employer to further exploit them. Many of the children are sexually and physically abused. Jonathan Blagbrough [**Note 19**]

Note 16: Use of a specific example involving an individual also makes an effective appeal to *Pathos*, as it personalizes the issue more.

Note 17: While you should introduce experts to your readers, you do not need to introduce ordinary journalists—just make sure to cite the information.

Note 18: In MLA format papers, we only use numerals in the body of papers for 100 and over (unless we are directly quoting).

Note 19: Introduce expert sources to your audience. Your readers should know why the sources you choose are credible. Generally, it is more effective to tall

◀ WRITING LOGICAL AND EFFECTIVE ▶

has a Master's degree in International, European and Comparative Law and is currently working as an independent consultant on child exploitation issues. [**Note 20**] He states, "The child's isolated situation coupled with her ambiguous role in the employers' household makes her particularly vulnerable to physical, verbal and sexual abuse" (186). Male members of the family use them for their sexual pleasure, and if they become pregnant, they are thrown out in the street. Their families shun the victims, who usually end up forced to become prostitutes in order to survive (186).

The online sexual exploitation of children is another form of human sex trafficking. Traffickers live-stream the sexual abuse of children using web cameras or Smartphones, with viewers paying to watch. Modern technologies enable predators to "target, recruit, and coerce children to engage in sexual activity." Tens of thousands of children, both girls and boys, are sexually exploited online around the world. ("Trafficking in Persons Report 2017" 32). Parents need to be vigilant and monitor their children's online activity, as well as being on the alert for signs of exploitation, such as isolation and depression and not wanting family members to see their cell phones. [**Note 21**]

Debt bondage is another form of modern slavery. People are forced to work more than twelve hours a day, paid little or no wages, and, when paid wages, are subject to illegal deductions from their meager paychecks to cover the cost

---

your readers why a person is considered an expert—the name titles of articles and books, etc., are available on the works cited page, and titles alone don't give detailed information on a person's expertise.

Note 20: Establishing a source's expertise furthers the student's appeal to *Logos*—to logic and credible evidence.

Note 21: Following cited information with commentary provides an effective end to the paragraph.

of equipment, materials, clothing, and interest on their loans. [**Note 22**] As a result, it is virtually impossible to ever repay the loans, and the loans can be passed to other members of the family for generations. In countries like India, poverty-stricken families are coerced into selling their children to moneylenders as collateral for their debts. The children are then made to work more than fourteen hours a day. They are beaten and burned if they do not meet the quotas and compensated less than fifty cents a week. These families are illiterate and easily manipulated by unethical moneylenders (Boutros 5). Heidi Boutros is an anti-slavery activist who engaged in independent research on debt bondage in India while working with the International Justice Mission. Debt bondage depends on unethical, exploitive agreements that trap people in a widespread, even open type of slavery, leaving them feeling entirely helpless and hopeless. She states,

> Only rarely does a written agreement between the laborer and their *mudalali*, which is someone who makes their living by buying and selling, detail how much money was borrowed, how much interest will be charged, and other relevant information. These factors allow *mudalalis* to manipulate interest rates and other details to force laborers to work well after the value of the laborers' work has exceeded the amount of the advance. (Boutros 5) [**Note 23**]

Note 22: The student doesn't forget to keep her imagined audience in mind throughout her paper. She doesn't take for granted that they understand all of the terms that she uses when discussing her topic. Keeping the appeal to *Logos* in mind, when editing her paper, she asked herself, "Have I defined all important terms that my audience might not understand?

Note 23: Since this quotation is over four lines long, it is indented one inch from the left margin and quotation marks are omitted. With indented direct quotations, periods precede the citations.

◀ WRITING LOGICAL AND EFFECTIVE ▶

Boutros observed many instances of debt bondage first hand and the terrible impact it has on families. It is wide spread and not really hidden; it is a generations-old tradition of exploitation.

While it is easy for Americans to imagine slavery in other countries, particularly poorer ones, slavery is happening right under our own noses. Writer Stephanie Hepburn and Rita Simon, of the School of Public Affairs, Washington College of Law, American University, Washington, write, "The U.S. is one of the top 10 destinations for human trafficking—with tens of thousands of people trafficked into the country each year. There have been reports of trafficking in over 90 U.S. cities" (1). [**Note 24**] Human trafficking in the U.S. is happening all around us—we simply don't know how to see it.

Someone made to work because of being threatened by beatings is classified as a slave. Forced labor is more common in Asia and the Pacific regions, but it also occurs in countries like Canada, the U.S., and Japan. It has been estimated that over ten to twelve million people are in forced labor and that approximately half are under the age of eighteen. Many become victims of forced labor through trafficking or deception. Domestic servitude is a term used for one type of forced labor. In 2016, an Iraqi couple who settled in California enslaved an Indonesian domestic worker in their home. They held her legal documents so that she could not return and physically threatened her. She was forced to work sixteen to eighteen hours a day, with no days off and no regular pay. The woman, who had been brought to the United States by the couple illegally, didn't speak any English, and she only gained her freedom by slipping a nurse a plea for help in her native language

---

Note 24: Appeals to *Logos* involve providing factual data and statistics.

◀ PART FOUR ▶

(Zavadski). [**Note 25**] It is estimated that many of the thousands of enslaved people in the United States are held under the same conditions. [**Note 26**]

Considering the worldwide prevalence and number of victims of modern slavery, it would seem an impossible task to stop or even reduce this horrendous practice. There are, however, methods being used by individuals, organizations, and countries that are helping victims of trafficking. Kevin Bales is the co-founder and former president of Free the Slaves, as wells as Professor of Contemporary Slavery at the Wilberforce Institute for the Study of Slavery and Emancipation, University of Hull, UK. Free the Slaves is an international non-governmental organization (NGO) and lobbying group created to campaign against slavery around the world. The group's strategy is based on the idea that slavery can best be abolished if people can meet their basic needs. Free the Slaves believes that people must have access to education, economic opportunities, and health services, as well as being protected by a strong rule of law. These are the basic factors needed to reduce the vulnerability of poor people to slavery ("Mission Statement"). Bales explains the three steps that can help eradicate slavery. He strongly advocates joining anti-slavery organizations and supporting those organizations with actions and funds. [**Note 27**]

Note 25: The second use of a specific example involving an individual also personalizes the issue more.

Note 26: The student reminds her audience that what happened to the individual woman she just mentioned is also happening to thousands of others—and they have not yet been freed, an effective appeal to *Pathos*.

Note 27: The student has not forgotten that she needs to let her readers know what they, as ordinary citizens, can do to help combat the problems she discusses. This also furthers an appeal to *Ethos*, as the discussions of solutions strengthen her presentation as a concerned and responsible person—and the

◀ WRITING LOGICAL AND EFFECTIVE ▶

> Groups like Anti-Slavery International, Free the Slaves, and Amnesty International follow one effective path. Watching and listening, studying and monitoring, they investigate abuses of human rights by corrupt regimes. They are dedicated to in-depth, factual, and responsible reporting of abuses. They then make it their business to carry those reports both to the public and to international bodies. (Bales 247) [**Note 28**]

Bales states that The "Rugmark campaign" has also been a success. Formed in 1994, the Rugmark Foundation comprises the following business associations and human rights organizations: the Carpet Manufacturers' Association Without Child Labor, the Indo-German Export Promotion Council, UNICEF India and their partners in the international anti-slavery movement, and the South Asian Coalition on Children in Servitude. In order to be able to attach a Rugmark label, the carpet maker has to agree to not participate in child enslavement or forced labor, to agree to monitoring by the Rugmark Foundation, and must also agree to paying one percent of carpet wholesale profits to any form of welfare fund for child workers. The Rugmark Foundation also requires regular school attendance by children who are working at home on their families' looms. Many mail order companies and big retailers in this country and other large countries now import only Rugmarked carpets (Bales 241).

---

suggestion that she sees her readers as also being concerned and responsible people.

Note 28: The student has effectively presented empirical data from experts throughout her paper, making *Logos* the dominant appeal. This is appropriate for a research paper.

◀ PART FOUR ▶

Many countries have enacted legislation to combat slavery and trafficking. President Clinton signed the Trafficking Victims Protections Act of 2000 into law on October 16, 2000. According to Kara C. Ryf, a labor and employment attorney, the act covers the prevention, protection and prosecution of trafficking victims. It provides for assistance to countries that meet the minimum requirements of the act. The countries must ban trafficking and arrest those who engage in trafficking, and make a serious effort to eliminate trafficking. If they do not meet these requirements, they will receive economic sanctions (Ryf 54).

Even more recently, Congress has taken action. In 2016, Congress passed the End Modern Slavery Initiative, which was legislation introduced by Senate Foreign Relations Committee Chairman Bob Corker. When he signed the bill into law on December 23, 2016, Corker stated,

> As I have seen firsthand, the stark reality of modern slavery is unconscionable, demanding the United States and civilized world make a commitment to end it for good. By providing strong U.S. leadership and leveraging our limited foreign aid dollars, this initiative will work with foreign governments and philanthropic organizations to match the funding being provided by the United States and create a coordinated effort to implement best practices to eliminate modern slavery and human trafficking around the globe. (Holtman)

We can credit Congress for bipartisan support of the End Modern Slavery Initiative and its signing into law, but we must also credit the ordinary citizens who lobbed their senators and representatives to support this bill, and we should never forget that the battle isn't over yet.

◀ WRITING LOGICAL AND EFFECTIVE ▶

Even before the End Modern Slavery Initiative was signed into law, the United States Department of State created the Office to Monitor and Combat Trafficking in Persons. The Office's website has several extremely helpful pages, including "Fifteen Ways You Can Help Fight Human Trafficking." [**Note 29**] It provides a great deal of information, including the following: [**Note 30**]

Human Trafficking Indicators

While not an exhaustive list, these are some key red flags that could alert you to a potential trafficking situation that should be reported:

- Living with employer
- Poor living conditions
- Multiple people in cramped space
- Inability to speak to individual alone
- Answers appear to be scripted and rehearsed
- Employer is holding identity documents
- Signs of physical abuse
- Submissive or fearful
- Unpaid or paid very little
- Under eighteen and in prostitution

Note 29: The student strengthens her paper by providing more information on what they can do—and taking it from a very credible source. This is concrete, practical information. The student never simply resorts to "wishful thinking."

Note 30: Only use colons in sentences after independent clauses. Do not use a colon simply bcause a phrase introduces a sentence element, such as a series. If the student had written, "It provides a great deal of information, including" she would not use a colon.

◀ PART FOUR ▶

Questions to Ask

Assuming you have the opportunity to speak with a potential victim privately and without jeopardizing the victim's safety because the trafficker is watching, here are some sample questions to ask to follow up on the red flags you became alert to:

- Can you leave your job if you want to?
- Can you come and go as you please?
- Have you been hurt or threatened if you tried to leave?
- Has your family been threatened?
- Do you live with your employer?
- Where do you sleep and eat?
- Are you in debt to your employer?
- Do you have your passport/identification? Who has it?

The web page, located at https://www.state.gov/j/tip/id/help, also gives readers the names of departments and agencies to contact and useful phone numbers, including the National Human Trafficking Resource Center, a national twenty-four hour, multilingual, toll-free anti-trafficking hotline. The Center takes calls from over the United States from "potential trafficking victims, community members, law enforcement, medical professionals, legal professionals, service providers, researchers, students, and policymakers" and others ("Fifteen Ways You Can Help ").

[**Note 31**] Modern slavery, in all its many forms, affects millions of people worldwide. It is imperative that we combine our efforts to eliminate

---

Note 31: The student doesn't make the mistake that so many student writers do—beginning her concluding paragraph with the boring, redundant phrase "in conclusion." She also refrained from introducing any new information in

this practice because of the immense suffering of the victims. We all have the responsibility to educate ourselves about modern slavery. It is important that everyone knows who are the most vulnerable, how they are kidnapped or recruited, and how to identify and prosecute traffickers. People can join and support anti-slavery organizations even if they cannot actively participate in other ways to end trafficking. These organizations help to prevent others from succumbing to the traps that slavers employ by supporting anti-slavery legislation and activities around the world and through education. They also help to pay off the debts for the victims of debt slavery. It may be a huge task, but with enough concerned people donating their time and energy, we have the potential of abolishing modern day slavery.

---

her conclusion, recognizing that anything like that belongs in the body of the paper. Her conclusion provides a sense of closure to the paper, highlighting the key points that she has made in support of her thesis. It mirrored her introduction, where she told readers what she planned to prove and the information that she would cover, but she didn't simply repeat herself. Also, she ended the paper with a strong, optimistic assertion.

◀ PART FOUR ▶

Works Cited

Bales, Kevin. *Disposable People: New Slavery in the Global Economy*. U of California P, 2012. [**Note 32**]

Blagbrough, Jonathan. "Child Domestic Labour: A Modern Form of Slavery." *Children and Society*, vol. 22, no. 3, May 2008, pp. 179-90. *Academic Search Premier*, doi: 10.1111/j. 1099-0860.2008.00149.x. [**Note 33**]

Boutros, Heidi. "India's Modern Slaves: Bonded Labor in India and Methods of Intervention." *Frontiers: The Interdisciplinary Journal of Study Abroad*, vol. 12, Nov. 2005, 1–26. *Eric*, eric.ed.gov/?id=EJ891472. [**Note 34**]

Celizic, Mike. "Teen Recounts Horror of Abduction into Sex Slavery." *NBCNEWS*, 13 Nov. 2008, www.today.com/news/teen-recounts-horror-abduction-sex-slavery-1C9013941. [**Note 35**]

Note 32: Remember that all entries on a Works Cited page should begin with the authors' last names first (if the authors' names are provided). We use authors' last names to put the entries into alphabetical order. If there are two authors, do not reverse the first and last names of the second author. If there are three or more, you only need the first author, followed by a comma and "et al."

Note 33: Make sure that you use current, not obsolete, MLA format. Formerly, volume and issue numbers, years, and pages for academic journals were presented like this, and months and seasons were omitted: 22.3 (2008): 179-90. In April 2016, the eight edition of *The MLA Handbook* as released. This was a committee effort, and the format for publications information for journals was has changed to this: vol. 22, no. 3 May 2008, pp. 179-90.

Note 34: In this and other entries in your papers, it is important to remember that articles (also essays, short stories, poems, and songs) are enclosed in quotation marks. Names of journals and other periodicals, books, plays, databases, and websites are italicized. Nothing is ever both enclosed in quotation marks and italicized.

Note 35: Remember that months over four letters long are abbreviated on works cited pages. Do not forget periods and spaces after abbreviations. The standard abbreviation for September should be used: Sept. (Databases often just have Sep.

◀ WRITING LOGICAL AND EFFECTIVE ▶

"Fifteen Ways You Can Help Fight Human Trafficking." United States Department of State, Office to Monitor and Combat Trafficking in Persons, www.state.gov/j/tip/id/help. [**Note 36**]

"Harriet Tubman." *Biography.com*, www.biography.com/people/harriet-tubman-9511430.

Hepburn, Stephanie, and Rita Simon. "Hidden in Plain Sight: Human Trafficking in the United States." *Gender Issues*, vol. 27, no. 1, June 2010, pp. 1-26. *Academic Search Premier*, doi: 10.1007/s12147-010-9087-7. [**Note 37**]

"Mission Statement." *Free the Slaves*, www.freetheslaves.net/about-us/mission-vision-history.

Ryf, Kara C. "The First Modern Anti-Slavery Law: The Trafficking Victims Protections Act of 2000." *Case Western Reserve Journal of International Law* vol. 34, no. 1, Winter 2002, pp. 45-71. Business Source Elite, ezproxy.bakersfieldcollege.edu: 2105/ehost/resultsadvanced?vid=7&sid=fc062743-1c29-4b70-83b3-e2038 84feca8%40sessionmgr4006&bquery=Ryf%2c+-

---

Don't use that). When entries end with URLs, use your word processing program to remove the hyperlink so that the URL doesn't print out blue and underlined.

Note 36: Individual authors are not always given. When a work is published by an organization, agency, government entity, etc., that is also its "author," so we omit just begin with the title of the work. We simply list the agency, etc., after the title as the publisher. We put the work in alphabetical order on the page by the first important word of the title. That simply means that if a work begins with "A," "An," or "The," we leave it in place, but we ignore it when we are putting the list of works cited entries into proper order.

Note 37: Use p. if front of the page number if the work is on one page only, and use pp. in front of numbers for works on two or more pages. When page numbers are in the same range of a hundred or a thousand (but not under 100), drop the first numeral of the last page number..

◀ PART FOUR ▶

Kara+C&bdata=JmRiPWJzaCZ0eXBlPTEmc2l0ZT1laG9zdC1saXZlJn-Njb3BlPXNpdGU%3d. [**Note 38**]

"Trafficking in Persons Report 2017." U.S. Department of State, Office to Monitor and Combat Trafficking in Persons, www.state.gov/documents/organization/271339.pdf.

"What is Modern Slavery?" *Anti-Slavery International*, www.antislavery.org/slavery-today/modern-slavery. [**Note 39**]

Zavadski, Katie. "Feds: San Diego Couple Enslaved Their Maid." *The Daily Beast*, 10 Apr. 2016, www.thedailybeast.com/feds-san-diego-couple-enslaved-their-maid. [**Note 40**]

Note: 38: Current MLA format asks for URLs at the end of entries for websites. Check with your instructor--he or she may prefer that you simply use the word "web" instead of the URL.

Note 39: When a title ends with a qestion mark, do not add a period. Question marks and exclamation marks are also termnal punctuation marks.

Note 40: Most URLs begin with "http://" or "https://." However, you should omit that part.

◀ WRITING LOGICAL AND EFFECTIVE ▶

 ## Avoiding Faulty Arguments

Arguments are composed of premises and conclusions. In the discipline of logic, people talk about two types of errors in arguments: formal and informal fallacies.

 ## Formal Fallacies

A formal fallacy gets its name from the fact that it involves an error in the form, in other words, the structure of the argument. When we talk about argument structure, we are talking about deductive logic. A deductive argument is an argument that is intended be deductively valid, to provide a guarantee of the truth of a conclusion if the argument's premises are factually true. If a valid argument has true premises, then the argument is said to be sound. All deductive arguments are either valid or invalid, and either sound (both valid and factual) or unsound.

When looking for formal fallacies in deductive arguments, the point is not whether a conclusion is true or false, but whether the form of the argument is correct or incorrect; the technical terms are "valid" and "invalid."

The concluding statement of an argument may be true even though the argument is formally invalid, and to the concluding statement of an argument may be false even though the argument is formally valid.

Formally Valid Arguments:

True and Valid:

> All humans are mortal.
> Sarah is a human.
> Therefore, Sarah is mortal.

False but Valid:

> All humans are werewolves.
> Sarah is a human.
> Therefore, Sarah is a werewolf.

The above argument is valid—in fact, it has exactly the same form as the preceding argument. However, the premises are false, so it does not matter that the conclusion follows logically from them.

False and Invalid:

> Some humans are vampires.
> Pierre is a human.
> Therefore, Pierre is a vampire.

The above argument would be valid (though still false) if the first premise said that all humans are vampires, not just some.

True but Invalid:

> Some humans are mortal.
> Sarah is a human.
> Therefore, Sarah is mortal.

"Some humans are mortal" is literally true because all humans are mortal. However, because the first premise, only asserts "some," the argument is technically invalid. Look at the same argument form, also with true premises, but with an untrue conclusion:

> Some humans are male.
> Sarah is a human.
> Therefore, Sarah is a male.

Formal fallacies present invalid arguments where the concluding statement does not necessarily follow from the statements preceding it. The conclusion may be objectively true, but its truth does not depend on or follow from its premises.

 INFORMAL FALLACIES

Inductive reasoning is different from deductive reasoning because we do not focus on the formal structure of the arguments. In fact, inductive reasoning is what we do most of the time—inductive reasoning makes generalizations from observations. We look at information, and then we draw conclusions.

◀ WRITING LOGICAL AND EFFECTIVE ▶

As far as deductive reasoning goes, the most famous practitioner in fiction is Sherlock Holmes, the character created by Sir Arthur Conan Doyle. Holmes is famous for his brilliant deductions. The only problem is that most of his arguments and the conclusions he reaches are, in fact, examples of inductive reasoning. For example, in *The Hound of the Baskervilles*, he explains exactly how he knew it had to be Dr. Watson who had been in the moor: "I could not undertake to recognize your footprint amid all the footprints in the world. If you seriously desire to deceive me you must change your tobacconist; for when I see the stub of a cigarette marked Bradley, Oxford Street, I know that my friend Watson is in the neighborhood" (148). Watson's love for the cigarettes manufactured by Bradley, however, doesn't mean there is no other possible person who could have been in the moor—presumably, Watson is not the only customer who buys that brand. A business would fail pretty quickly with just one customer. Holmes generalized from an observation, but it is Doyle's craft that makes him always right—not the form of all of his arguments. With Holmes, it is mainly both induction and intuition, not deduction.

In real life, if the premises can effectively support a conclusion, then an argument is considered strong. If the premises do not adequately support the conclusion, then the argument is considered weak or fallacious. With inductive logic, we do not use the terms valid and invalid or sound and unsound. Instead, we examine the strength of the evidence, the types of evidence offered, the relationship between what is offered as evidence to the actual conclusions drawn, and whether the conclusions logically follow the premises. Following is a list of common informal fallacies that you should avoid when constructing your arguments and that you should be able to recognize when reading or listening to other people's arguments.

 ## COMMON INFORMAL FALLACIES

The **anecdotal evidence fallacy** happens when someone ignores or minimizes empirical evidence in favor of personal stories that may be compelling sounding but are actually unrepresentative. This is also called the "confabulation fallacy."

Example: Smoking isn't as dangerous as many people claim—my grandfather started smoking when he was fourteen, up to three packs a day, and he lived to be ninety-six.

Appeal to authority is the fallacy of saying that simply because an authority or someone passed off as an authority supports something, it must be true—or if such a person attacks something, it must be untrue. Authorities can disagree. Sometimes a so-called "authority" isn't really an expert in the field all. Sometimes authorities prostitute themselves for money from corporations, such as the scientists who worked for the tobacco industry and suppressed evidence that smoking was both harmful and addictive, enabling tobacco industry executives to give sworn statements to Congress—even though they knew they were lying.

Example: I am not going to vaccinate my children. I don't want them to get autism. Dr. Andrew Wakefield conducted research that proves that there is a connection between autism and the MMR vaccine.

Appeal to consequences takes the form of saying we should accept conclusions that are psychologically comfortable to us and reject conclusions if they cause us psychological discomfort. This is related to what psychologists call "confirmation bias," which is the tendency to seek, prefer, interpret, and remember information in a way that confirms our preexisting beliefs.

Example: I don't believe that human actions contribute to climate change. I can't do anything about it anyway, and I don't want to change the way that I live. I love my SUV.

Appeal to ignorance argues that if we cannot prove that something is false, it must be true, or the other way around.

Example: I believe in ghosts—no one has ever been able to prove that they don't exist.

Appeal to the moon doesn't involve making an appeal to the moon itself. It argues that the history of scientific inventions ensures that in the future, someone will always be able to figure out a solution to any problems that we face, so we really don't need to worry about the problems that we are facing or creating now. "If we can put a man on the moon, we must also be able to . . . ."

Example: I don't worry about climate change. After all, if scientists can put a man on the moon, they can surely figure out how to deal with these other problems before it's too late.

◀ WRITING LOGICAL AND EFFECTIVE ▶

Appeal to ridicule happens when, instead of producing evidence for or against something, a position or the advocate of a position is ridiculed and sometimes even misrepresented.

Example: Of course I don't believe in evolution—the idea that monkeys and other apes are going to "evolve" into human beings is stupid.

Appeal to tradition, also called the "traditional wisdom fallacy," argues that something must be accepted as good because it is traditional or rejected as bad because it is not. This resembles "appeal to popularity," but it focuses on the past.

Example: It was a mistake to elect Sadiq Khan the mayor of London—London never had a Muslim mayor before, and his family wasn't even English—they came from Pakistan.

Arguments against the person, also called "ad hominem fallacies," involve some type of attack on people making an argument, not on the real arguments.

> **Abusive ad hominem** happens when someone simply attacks an opponent as immoral, unintelligent, or something else bad.
>
> *Example: I'm not buying that argument about sexual harassment being a big problem—it's just a lot of nasty women making things up because they can't do their jobs well.*
>
> The **bad reasons fallacy** involves concluding that an opponent's conclusion is entirely wrong because he or she provided bad reasons. If all the reasons used to back up a conclusion are bad, then it is logical to reject the conclusion. But sometimes people who are right about something make some poor arguments. They may even be right for the wrong reasons. We cannot justifiably reject an entire conclusion simply because one or more people who believe it provide bad reasons for believing it.
>
> *Example: I am not going to vote in favor of increasing funding for the public library. My neighbor was saying how she was going to vote for it because she knows the people campaigning for that measure and they are really great people. That is a really stupid reason to vote for something.*

Circumstantial ad hominem arguments attack other people's arguments by claiming that circumstances affecting the people making the argument make their arguments worthless. While we should pay attention to conflicts of interest and other potentially relevant factors, arguments should be judged on their own merits, not simply dismissed because of the situations of some of the people making the argument.

Example: I don't agree with you that the sciences need funding at the level they have been getting—after all, you are a scientist, so of course you'd say the sciences need more funding.

Poisoning the well happens when a person argues that we can totally disregard the arguments offered by those with opposing viewpoints because they allegedly cannot be trusted to tell the truth. Such a fallacy metaphorically says that "anything that comes out of that well is poisoned"—in other words, anything that person says is flawed just because he or she says it, so disregard it. It is often used as an excuse to avoid arguments that the other side uses that are too strong to effectively refute.

Example: Don't bother to look at that crooked, sleazy goofball's so-called "proof"—nothing he comes up with can be trusted.

The **tu quoque fallacy** (translated as "you, also" or "you're another") occurs when someone mounts a defense against criticism by accusing an opponent of being guilty of the same wrongdoing. Whether the other person is indeed guilty of the same or a similar wrong is irrelevant to the truth of the original charge.

Example: How can you accuse me creating fake news when one of your own stories was proven false last week?

Begging the question happens when the conclusion of an argument is reworded and presented as a premise instead of offering a genuine premise in support of the argument. It is also called "circular reasoning" and "the vicious circle."

Example: Marriage between same-sex couples should not be legal because marriage is only supposed to be between a man and a woman.

Common Practice happens when someone justifies wrongdoing by claiming that a lot of other people engage in the same wrong. It asks the audience to accept that something wrong is excusable because a lot of people engage in the activity.

Example: So I copied most of my paper from a friend's paper—it saved me time, and lots of other students do it. Everybody knows that.

False cause happens when someone claims that something that follows something else or that occurs with it must be caused by it. Sometimes the relationship is just coincidental. Sometimes both are caused by something else not yet identified. Sometimes there is a cause-effect relationship, but it may be the reverse of the suggested relationship.

Example: Black cats are bad luck. My sister got a black cat a few months ago, and since then, someone stole her purse, one of her tires blew out, and she got strep throat. I keep telling her she has to get rid of that cat!

A **false dilemma** is produced when someone insists that there are only two possible options available, when there may be more—or when the two choices are not mutually exclusive. It is also called "false dichotomy," the "black and white fallacy," and the "either-or fallacy." Usually the arguer presents a choice that seems attractive and contrasts it with something extreme and unattractive (and probably unlikely) that few people would think of as acceptable. This also occurs when people try to defend actions in the past by stating something that they believe to be true, or is partially true, or even totally true, and asserting, de facto, that another thing that simultaneously occurred could not have happened.

Example: We have to either support public funding of private schools or only support failing schools. There are no other choices.

The **hasty generalization** fallacy occurs when an argument is defended based on insufficient samples, unrepresentative samples, or a combination of the both.

Example: I am sure that measure is going to be defeated—almost everybody who phoned into a radio program I was listening to yesterday said they are going to vote against it.

Invincible ignorance happens when someone insists on the legitimacy of a position in spite of overwhelming evidence against it.

Example: I smoke in my house and in my car with my kids around because I just don't see how "second hand smoke" could hurt anybody—after all, they aren't the ones smoking. I don't care what those so-called "experts" say.

The **opinion entitlement fallacy** happens when an individual asserts the right to have an opinion as if that right alone presents a logical defense of the opinion. This is often the last resort of people who see all the premises they use to bolster their claims get dismantled. With nothing left, they fall back on the assertion that "I am entitled to my own opinion!" This is a fact in a democracy—but it is not, however, a premise that can support any argument (at least ones unrelated to arguments about freedom of speech).

Example: I don't care what evidence you have—I have the right to my own opinion, and no one can take that away from me.

Red Herring is the fallacy of bringing up issues or examples that are irrelevant but emotional and compelling enough to distract the audience from the real point. The audience may be swayed because the issue may be emotionally very powerful to them, so they miss the fact that it is logically irrelevant to the argument.

Example: Critics accuse our candidate of unethical conduct, but let's not forget the really major problems our country is facing right now—the middle class is shrinking, crime is growing, the infrastructure is crumbling—we need to focus on real problems and to do something about them right now!

The **slippery slope** fallacy argues that a sequence of increasingly unacceptable events will follow from an action or event that may not in itself seem unreasonable until the arguer takes us all the way to something no reasonable person would want to see occur. "False dilemma" ignores middle grounds and alternatives, while the slippery slope fallacy acknowledges middle grounds but moves from one point at the beginning to an unpleasant extreme at the other end. A may be next to B, and so on, but that does not mean that A will inevitably move you to Z.

◀ WRITING LOGICAL AND EFFECTIVE ▶

Example: Sure, we could raise the mandatory minimum wage by two and a half dollars, but then what? If we do that, next people will be asking that we raise it another two and a half dollars, then five dollars more, then even more. Pretty soon we'll have most businesses going bankrupt because employers won't be able to afford to pay their workers forty or fifty dollars an hour, and then where will the country be?

The **straw person** fallacy occurs when someone attacks an exaggerated, distorted, or even entirely false version of an opponent's argument instead of dealing with the real evidence that the opponent offers. It gets its name because it would be a lot easier to defeat a person made of straw instead of a real person in a fight—especially a stronger one.

Example: You say you agree with a vaccine advisory panel that recommends that all girls and women between the ages of eleven and twenty-six should receive a vaccine that will prevent most cases of cervical cancer. However, this cancer is related to sexual activity, and I think it is really evil of you to promote sexual activity in little girls!

A **weak analogy** happens when an argument is based on an analogy—a comparison—that is so weak that the argument is too weak to adequately support a conclusion. For an argument based on an analogy to be effective, the issues, objects, etc. being compared should have strongly relevant similarities and no relevant dissimilarities.

Example: The universe is like a watch—both are complex and both run. A watch has to have a designer, so the universe must have an intelligent designer, too.

PART FIVE

UNDERSTANDING & AVOIDING PLAGIARISM

 ## Understanding and Avoiding Plagiarism

Rory had his new girlfriend, Amy, come over one night when his roommate was away for the weekend because he wanted to cook her dinner and impress her with his culinary skills. (At least that's his story, and he's sticking to it.) In the middle of cooking, he realized that he didn't have any mushrooms, so he dug into his roommate's stash in the fridge and took some of his. Rory left a note that said he'd replace the produce when he went shopping next. The meal was a success, the roommate knew he'd get his mushrooms replaced when he got home and read the note, and everyone was happy (especially because Rory also cleaned up the kitchen and did the dishes). The next weekend, the roommate was gone again, so Rory had Amy come over again. This time, he realized he was out of pasta and took some from his roommate's shelf in the pantry, but without leaving a note. This meal went over well, too, but when his roommate came home from soccer practice hungry a few days later, he was very upset to face a spaghetti dinner without any spaghetti.

Writing is like cooking. You are trying to put something successful together, so you need to get the right ingredients. Where you get the ingredients matters, especially if you are taking them from someone else. Pasta is obviously not an idea, but the theft of the pasta is no different than the theft of what we call "intellectual property." If you take someone's ideas without giving them credit and leaving a citation (the academic equivalent of a note), you are plagiarizing. All types of plagiarism are not equal, however. Following are five common types:

◀ PART FIVE ▶

 TYPES OF PLAGIARISM

1. **Total Plagiarism** occurs when students turn in other people's work and pretend they wrote it. It is intentional dishonesty and might involve an entire paper copied or purchased off the Web, work written by another student, or a paper hobbled together from more than one work. Such papers may have language changed and citations added to try to disguise the fraud, but such additions do not change the basic truth: the student has stolen work rather than writing it.

   This is the type of plagiarism that can result in academic probation, failing classes, and other official punitive responses. It is also fairly easy for professors to catch (even without anti-plagiarism services like Turnitin.com). Some students forget that anything they can find, their professors can find—often faster. Also, professors usually have a better understanding of students' writing styles than the students themselves. What may look like a clever move to the student may scream, "I stole this paper!!!" on the first page once the instructor starts reading it.

2. **Substantial Plagiarism** occurs when students do most of the writing in their own papers but (1) borrow numerous exact phrases and sentences without enclosing them in quotation marks (or using block quotations when applicable) and without giving credit to the original source—which is as dishonest as total plagiarism, (2) borrow ideas and rephrase them without giving credit to the original source, or (3) borrow exact phrases and sentences without enclosing them in quotation marks (or using block quotations) even though credit is given to the original source. These acts of plagiarism are also deliberate and blatant and grounds for failure or other sanctions.

3. **Incidental/occasional Plagiarism** occurs when students write their own papers, but there are sections that will not withstand strict scrutiny. For example, one or more passages may have exact quotations of sentences and phrases that are not correctly indicated as direct quotations, even though the information is attributed to the sources. Students may also create one or more passages where paraphrased

◀ UNDERSTANDING & AVOIDING PLAGIARISM ▶

ideas are not attributed to their sources. Sometimes plagiarism in this category is accidental because the student does not understand how to properly paraphrase.

4. **Buddy/tutor Plagiarism** occurs when students get too much help from friends or tutors. In some cases, the friend or tutor may rewrite entire sections (or all) of the paper. It is wise to have someone else look at your paper, but don't allow them to help you rewrite any of it. Use another person's input to help you find technical errors or to alert you to areas that aren't clear, but do the rewriting yourself. Also, if you team up with a friend from class and work together, it is a good idea to produce your own work—don't both submit the same exact assignment, or it will appear as if one of you may have cheated.

5. **Accidental Plagiarism** occurs when students don't realize that using other people's ideas and paraphrasing them is plagiarism if the source is not clearly identified. This is perhaps the most common form of plagiarism and can be corrected with proper citations and documentation format. It can also occur when people haven't been careful when taking notes and forget to put quotation marks around direct quotations, or they polish up the paraphrased language of an attributed source and accidentally rephrase it into the original language of the source without adding quotation marks.

 RULES FOR AVOIDING PLAGIARISM

There are three rules for avoiding plagiarism, the first of which is pretty obvious:

Rule 1: Be honest. Don't buy, borrow, or steal anybody else's words or ideas.

Anything a student can find on a website, an instructor can find, too. The consequences are serious—students caught plagiarizing can face disciplinary action from their college or university, which can become part of their permanent records. And, of course, students who are caught plagiarizing generally earn failing grades on the assignments. Sometimes students feel they have to plagiarize because they have not managed their time well. Failing an assignments or an entire course is not a very cost-effective form of time management.

Rule 2: Cite *all* material that you take from a nonfiction source, whether you quote, paraphrase, or summarize, unless it is "common knowledge."

Sometimes students think they only have to cite direct quotations. That is a mistake—they have to identify and cite the ideas, whether they quote or not.

When you summarize ideas, you find the main ideas in a passage, section, or entire work and you rephrase them and condense the most important of these ideas in the source material and put them into your own words. The purpose of summarizing is to give the reader an overview of the passage, section, or entire work. You do not need to include examples, extra explanations, or background that the writer includes along with the main ideas.

When you paraphrase ideas, you convey all the information in the original passage in your own words. A paraphrase, unlike a summary, will be as long as the original—or even longer. You may need to clarify technical language other information, and that may take more words than the original passage, which may have been written to a specialized audience, not the general audience that you should be imagining. While you probably won't be writing a paper about tennis, that sport gives us an example. Suppose you paraphrased a passage describing an exciting tennis game, and someone wrote that the players scored deuce. You'd need more than one word to convey what "deuce" meant to people who know don't know the jargon.

If you are writing an essay about a single work of literature, however, the convention is to cite page numbers only for direct quotations from the work of literature, and not when you summarize or paraphrase any sections, but you still must cite all information you take from critical sources concerning the work of literature if you use other people's ideas.

Rule 3: Use language and sentence structures that are essentially your own.

Simply changing or rearranging a few words here and there isn't enough to avoid charges of stealing. For this reason, it is vital to master the art of paraphrasing.

◀ UNDERSTANDING & AVOIDING PLAGIARISM ▶

 EXAMPLES OF PLAGIARIZED AND UNPLAGIARIZED PARAGRAPHS

Following are examples of different types of plagiarism using part of a 1946 essay, "Politics and the English Language," written by British author George Orwell. Two examples of unplagiarized passages follow those.

This is the original passage from Orwell's essay:
> In our time it is broadly true that political writing is bad writing. Where it is not true, it will generally be found that the writer is some kind of rebel, expressing his private opinions and not a "party line." Orthodoxy, of whatever color, seems to demand a lifeless, imitative style. The political dialects to be found in pamphlets, leading articles, manifestos, White papers and the speeches of undersecretaries do, of course, vary from party to party, but they are all alike in that one almost never finds in them a fresh, vivid, homemade turn of speech.

Plagiarized Paragraph #1, with plagiarized words and phrases underlined:
> Today we find it basically <u>true that political writing is bad writing. Where it is not true, it</u> is because <u>the writer is some kind of rebel, stating his private opinions and not a 'party line'. Orthodoxy seems to demand a lifeless</u> and <u>imitative style. The political dialects differ from party to party, but they are all alike in that</u> we <u>almost never find in them a</u> new or <u>vivid</u> <u>turn of speech.</u>

The student who wrote the paragraph above is guilty of plagiarism for three reasons: 1) phrases are copied verbatim from the original but are not enclosed in quotation marks, 2) the original author is not given, and 3) there is no citation indicating the page number the material was taken from. The effect of the plagiarized material is to indicate that all the words and ideas are the student's own.

Plagiarized Paragraph #2, with plagiarized words and phrases underlined:
> Today it is mostly that case <u>that political writing is bad writing. Where</u> this <u>is not true, it will</u> usually <u>be found that the writer is</u> a <u>rebel, expressing his</u> own <u>opinions and not</u> the <u>"party line." Orthodoxy, of whatever</u> kind, results in a style that is neither vivid nor original. The language in various materials will be different depending on the political party

producing them, but they are all the same in the sense that we almost never find anything lively, fresh, original. (Orwell 178)

The preceding paragraph is also plagiarized because even though the author and page number appear in a parenthetical citation at the end of the sentence, phrases are copied verbatim from the original but are not enclosed in quotation marks. The effect of the plagiarized material is to indicate that although the ideas are Orwell's, all the words are the student's paraphrase of the original passage, which is clearly not the case.

Plagiarized Paragraph #3:

What do most examples of political writing have in common these days? It isn't any good. It is boring. It is unoriginal. It doesn't garb us. The few exceptions happen with writers who usually turn out to be conveying their own, individual ideas, not those of a political party or movement. It is certainly true that the actual ideas and stands taken by different parties and movements differ from each other a great deal. However, as noted earlier, the language used to express these differing ideas is uniformly dull and trite.

Although the paragraph above is an effective paraphrase, the student has still clearly plagiarized because (1) the source of the ideas is not given, and (2) there is no citation indicating the page number the material was taken from. The effect of the plagiarized material is to indicate that all the ideas are the student's own.

Unplagiarized Paragraph #1:

George Orwell, most well-know today for his dystopian novel 1984, wrote his famous essay "Politics and the English Language" in 1946. In his opinion, political writing, no matter how much the ideas of parties and movements differed, tended not to be very good writing. He felt that it was stale, boring, and unoriginal and that the few exceptions happened with writers who usually turned out to be conveying their own, individual ideas, not those of a political party or movement. It was true that the actual ideas and stands taken by different parties and movements differed from each other. However, the language used to express these differing ideas was, he felt, uniformly dull and trite. (178)

◀ UNDERSTANDING & AVOIDING PLAGIARISM ▶

This example is not plagiarized. The entire paragraph is put into the student's own words, and the passage ends with the correct MLA style parenthetical citation. Had the student not introduced Orwell immediately before the paraphrase, he or she would have needed to put Orwell's last name in front of the page number. You should always introduce sources the first time that you use them, but using their last names in citations is fine for later quotations, summaries, and paraphrases.

Unplagiarized Paragraph #2:

George Orwell wrote his famous essay "Politics and the English Language" in 1946. In his opinion, political writing, no matter how much the ideas of parties and movements differed, tended not to be very good writing. "Orthodoxy, of whatever color, seems to demand a lifeless, imitative style" (178). He felt that the few exceptions happened with writers who usually turned out to be conveying their own, individual ideas, not those of a political party or movement. He recognized that the actual ideas and stands taken by different parties and movements differed from each other. However, the language used was uniformly dull and trite. (178)

This example is not plagiarized. Most of the paragraph is put into the student's own words, and the passage contains parenthetical citations after both the quotation and the paraphrase.

 COMMON KNOWLEDGE EXCEPTIONS

The only source material that you can use without citing is material that is considered common knowledge and not attributable to just one source. **Common knowledge** refers to generally known facts that the average adult or educated reader knows, such as widely known dates and facts. Determining whether something should be considered common knowledge can be tricky, so cite a source if you're not sure. Also, be aware that information meeting the criteria for common knowledge doesn't mean that you can simply copy and paste sentences with this information from other people's work.

Here are examples of different types of common knowledge exceptions:

1. **Information known by the average person** (i.e., Aaron Burr killed Alexander Hamilton in a duel; the first African-American president was elected in 2008)

2. **Information known by the average scholar in a particular discipline** (i.e., William Shakespeare died in 1616 at the age of 52; Günter Grass won the Nobel Prize in Literature in 1999). Note that if you are writing for a class outside of that discipline, it will not be considered common knowledge and will likely need a citation.

3. **Information that is repeated in many different sources** (i.e., Various cancers are caused by inhaling or ingesting large amounts of toxic asbestos fibers.). "Many" is an ambiguous term, and there is no universal agreement on exactly how many sources it takes to make something "common knowledge," but the standard assumption in academia is that facts are common knowledge if you can find the same information reported in at least five different sources (it isn't a bad idea to ask your own professor for guidance).

To be safe, if you aren't sure if an idea is common knowledge, cite it! It is a lot safer to have a citation that you don't need than it is to risk an accusation of plagiarism. Don't be nervous and worry about "too many" citations. Writing research papers means that you are presenting research—you are supposed to have a lot of in-text citations.

PART SIX

BRIEF GUIDE TO PUNCTUATION & GRAMMAR

 IMPORTANT ELEMENTS OF PUNCTUATION AND GRAMMAR

Parts of Speech

The English language has eight major parts of speech: noun, pronoun, verb, adverb, adjective, conjunction, preposition, and interjection. You need to be able to distinguish between these in order to implement the rules for correctly punctuating sentences and to know which letters at the beginnings of words in titles and subtitles to capitalize and which not to.

Nouns

Nouns are the simplest parts of speech; they are the words used to name persons, animals, places, ideas, things, and events. They can be broken down into other categories, including proper nouns, which refer to specific persons and things and need to be capitalized, for example, "Yosemite," "United States" and "Statue of Liberty," and common nouns, which are simply the generic names of categories, such as "park," "country" and "monument."

Pronouns

Pronouns function as replacements for nouns, for example, "she," "he," and "it."

Verbs

Verbs could be considered the important part of a speech because without a verb, a sentence would not exist. A predicate is the portion of a clause that says something about the subject (who or what the clause is about). Every predicate must contain a verb. Verbs show physical or mental actions, such as "read," "write," "think," and "love," or states of being, for example, "am," is, "are, "was," and were."

Adjectives

Adjectives are the words that describe nouns and pronouns. We separate multiple adjectives from each other with commas, but we do not separate an adjective from the word that it is modifying with a comma. Examples of adjectives include the following: "incisive," "powerful," and "critical."

Adverbs

Like adjectives, adverbs are also used to describe words, but adverbs describe adjectives, verbs, or other adverb, for example, "very," "truly," and "deeply."

Some words can be both adjectives and adverbs, depending on how they are used. In the phrase "fast car," "fast" is an adjective modifying the noun "car." In the phrase "drive fast," "fast" is an adverb modifying the verb "drive."

Common Conjunctive Adverbs

Conjunctive adverbs are a particularly important type of adverb to recognize. They can connect clauses, providing useful transitions. They show relationships, such as contrast, sequence, and cause and effect. They may be moved around in the clause in which they appear.

accordingly	furthermore	moreover	similarly
also	hence	namely	still
anyway	however	nevertheless	the
besides	incidentally	next	thereafter
certainly	indeed	nonetheless	therefore,
consequently	instead	now	thus
finally	likewise	otherwise	undoubtedly
further	meanwhile		

Conjunctions

Conjunctions have several categories, including coordinating conjunctions and subordinating conjunctions.

◀ BRIEF GUIDE TO PUNCTUATION & GRAMMAR ▶

Coordinating Conjunctions

Coordinating conjunctions are used to join individual words, phrases, and independent clauses—units of equal "rank." You need to recognize them because their uses include connecting independent clauses, in which case they require a comma in front of them, and because they are words that we don't capitalize in titles or subtitles unless they being or end titles and subtitles. The seven coordinating conjunctions are "for," "and," "nor," "but," "or, "yet," and "so." You can use the mnemonic "FANBOYS" to remember all seven.

Subordinating Conjunctions

A subordinating conjunction joins a dependent clause (also called a subordinate clause) to an independent clause (also called a main clause). You need to recognize them because whether or not you use a comma with a dependent clause depends on whether it follows an impendent clause (no comma) or precedes it (use a comma between them). Following are some common subordinating conjunctions:

after	as though	in order that	that
although	because	lest (that)	though
as	before	now that	unless
as if	even if	provided	until
as long as	even though	since	when
as much as	if	so that	where
as soon as	inasmuch	than	wherever

Prepositions

Prepositions are words that express the relationship between two other nearby nouns or pronouns. You need to recognize them because they are words that we don't capitalize in titles or subtitles unless they being or end titles and subtitles. Following are some common prepositions:

about	behind	down	into
above	below	during	of
after	beneath	for	off

against	between	from	on
at	beyond	in	out
among	by	inside	with

Interjections

Interjections are words used to express feelings, for example, "ouch," "oops," and "uh oh."

Building Grammatical Sentences

Sentences are built of clauses and phrases. A clause has a **complete subject** and a **complete predicate**. The complete subject tells whom or what the sentence is about. The complete subject is who or what is "doing" the verb that is in the predicate, as well as all of the descriptive words that go with it, for example, "the best-selling author," "the year's most popular album," and "the latest craze." The simple subject is who or what that is "doing" the verb without any modifiers, for example, author, album, craze.

A predicate is the portion of a clause that says something about the subject. The complete predicate is the part that tells us tells what the subject does (or did, or will do) or is (or was, or will be). It includes a verb and all the other details that describe what is going on, for example, "spoke at our college last week," "won a Grammy award," "is a bit silly." The simple predicate is the main verb in the predicate that tells what the subject does, for example, "spoke," "won," "is."

A common commas error is separating a subject from its predicate with a comma if the complete subject and the complete predicate are rather long.

In the following examples, "cover-up" is the simple subject and the verb "preventing" is the simple predicate.

Incorrect:

There has been a persistent and deliberate cover-up, preventing the EPA from requiring the natural gas industry to make urgently needed reductions in methane venting and leakage across the nation's expanding natural gas infrastructure.

Correct:

There has been a persistent and deliberate cover-up preventing the EPA from requiring the natural gas industry to make urgently needed reductions in methane venting and leakage across the nation's expanding natural gas infrastructure.

Independent clauses, also called main clauses, can stand alone as sentence because they express complete thoughts. **Dependent clauses**, also called subordinate clauses, are dependent on independent clauses to make sense because they begin with subordinating words, most commonly, subordinating conjunctions.

Independent (main) clause:

> I love both Beyoncé and Adele.

Dependent (subordinate) clause:

> Because I love both Beyoncé and Adele

Obviously, you need to add an independent clause to the dependent clause to have a sentence that makes sense:

> Because I love both Beyoncé and Adele, I own all their albums.

Phrases are a lot like dependent clauses in that they cannot stand alone as sentences. They differ from clauses in that they lack either a subject, or a verb, or both, for example, "feeling brave," which has a verb but no subject. It needs to be attached to a main clause: "Feeling brave, I decided to try rock climbing." We punctuate them the same way we punctuate dependent clauses, though.

Sentences also have descriptive elements like **restrictive elements** (also called essential elements) and **nonrestrictive elements** (also called nonessential elements). They function as modifiers in sentences. A modifier is a word or group of words that describes or limits other words, phrases, and clauses. Restrictive elements are essential to the meaning of a sentence, but you can remove nonrestrictive element without changing meaning. We will discuss them and how to punctuate them later.

There are four types of sentences in the English language, any of which may also include phrases:

1. Simple sentences, which are made up of single independent clauses.
2. Compound sentences, which are made up of at least two independent clauses.
3. Complex sentences, which are made up of an independent clause and at least one dependent clause.
4. Compound-complex sentences, which are made up of two independent clauses and one or more dependent clauses.

Simple sentences are less error-prone because, well, they are so simple (though adding phrases can be a bit tricky). The most error-prone sentence types are the others because we combine independent clauses in different ways, and how we punctuate dependent clauses depends on where they are in their sentences.

Recognizing and Punctuating Independent (Main) Clauses

Compound sentences consist of consecutive independent clauses. There are three primary ways to punctuate consecutive independent clauses: with a period (or other terminal punctuation mark), with a comma in front of a coordinating conjunction, or with a semicolon. When you use a semicolon, it is usually inappropriate to follow it with a coordinating conjunction, but you can use a conjunctive adverb ("however," "therefore," "thus," "consequently" etc.) as a transitional device.

1. **Separate consecutive main clauses with a period or other terminal punctuation mark.**

    The term literacy has traditionally meant to ability to read and write. Media literacy is the ability to access and successfully evaluate many varieties of media.

    What is media literacy? It is the ability to access and successfully evaluate many varieties of media.

2. **Separate consecutive main clauses with a comma in front of a coordinating conjunction.**

◀ BRIEF GUIDE TO PUNCTUATION & GRAMMAR ▶

Media literacy is the ability to access and successfully evaluate many varieties of media, and people who are media literate are better able to objectively evaluate information and misinformation.

3. **Separate closely related consecutive main clauses with a semicolon.**

Media literacy is the ability to access and successfully evaluate many varieties of media; people who are media literate are better able to objectively evaluate information and misinformation.

If you use a conjunctive adverb as a transitional device, separate it from the clause it is in with commas. If it is at the beginning or end of a main clause, a semicolon or period can take the place of a comma.

Studies indicate that most Americans believe that they can differentiate between genuine news and fake news. The same studies, however, indicate that a significant number cannot.

Studies indicate that most Americans believe that they can differentiate between genuine news and fake news; however, the same studies indicate that a significant number cannot.

Some notes on semicolons:

A semicolon is often called a "weak period" because it acts exactly like a period does between two sentences. More importantly, when you use a semicolon, both sentences you combine with it must be on the same topic. If there isn't a logical connection between the two main clauses, don't use a semicolon. Below are two examples. The first example doesn't have a logical connection between the clauses, yet the second example does.

Illogical use: The man ran; I love the taste of coffee.

Logical use: I love the taste of coffee; I can't think of a better drink to wake up with.

Notice that the semicolon adds a slightly feeling to the sentence than a comma and a coordinating conjunction would or than splitting the sentence into two would.

As noted earlier, there are three primary ways of punctuating consecutive independent clauses. However, colons and dashes can also be used in some situations. Colons are used to introduce sentence elements, but only after independent clauses. In some cases, what they introduce are other independent clauses, as in the following example:

> Famed historian and linguist Noam Chomsky made the following observation: "Random exploration through the Internet turns out to be a cult generator."

Dashes are most commonly used to indicate shifts in tone and emphasis, and sometimes they can be used to do so between main clauses.

> The Internet can be very valuable if you know what you're looking for—but you need the ability to recognize crap when you encounter it.

Recognizing and Punctuating Dependent (Subordinate) Clauses

Complex and compound-complex sentences combine dependent clauses with independent clauses. How we punctuate a dependent clause depends on whether it precedes or follows an independent clause.

1. **When a dependent clause precedes an independent clause, separate the two with a comma.**

Complex sentence:

> While most people believe that they are objective and able to critically interpret information, confirmation bias is prevalent.

2. **Do not use a comma when a dependent clause follows an independent clause.**

Complex sentence:

> Critical thinking is the best way to solve problems because it requires looking at an issue from several standpoints before reaching a final decision.

Compound-complex sentence:

> While most people believe that they are objective and able to critically interpret information, confirmation bias is prevalent because it is usually entirely unconscious.

Basic Sentence Combining

Sentence combining can be thought of as the basic "math" of the English language. Once you master this system of sentence construction, you'll find that you've conquered the most common errors found in college-level writing. Sentence combining consists of patterns you'll use to construct different types of sentences to suit your needs as a writer. Think of it as building little Lego sentences, and you'll do just fine.

Using the punctuation rules described above, we can create sentences that are more sophisticated than a series of simple sentences. Writers who depend on only a series of simple sentences lay out a stream of thoughts that never seem to smoothly and effectively link or build on each other, and that's not very good writing. In fact, it comes across as childish. It isn't that simple sentences should be avoided—they are excellent, for example, for adding emphasis. Good writers vary sentence types. Consider the following paragraph, which is composed of a compound sentence, two complex sentences, another compound sentence, and ends with two simple sentences. The first of the two simple sentences is actually rather lengthy—it could be awkward to add it to another lengthy clause. We could simply add it to the last simple sentence, which is only two words long, but a semicolon or a comma with a coordinating conjunction would be less dramatic.

> Amelia Earhart was an American aviation pioneer and author, and she was the first female aviator to fly solo across the Atlantic Ocean. After she completed her flight across the Atlantic, she was awarded the U.S. Distinguished Flying Cross. She became a widely known international celebrity because she set many other records and wrote best-selling books about her experiences. She served at Purdue University as an advisor on aeronautical engineering; she was also a member of the National Woman's Party and an early supporter of the Equal Rights Amendment.

Earhart decided to try a circumnavigation flight around the globe in 1937 in a Purdue-funded Lockheed Model 10 Electra. She disappeared.

Common Sentence Combining Errors to Avoid

The three most common errors when looking at sentence combining are comma splices, run-ons, and fragments.

1. **Comma splices**

A comma splice consists of two independent clauses "spliced" together with a comma and no coordinating conjunction, for example,

> The Newseum opened in 2008, more than six million people have visited this museum on Pennsylvania Avenue between the United States Capitol and the White House.

This can be fixed by changing the comma to a period or semicolon or by adding the appropriate coordinating conjunction after the comma:

> The Newseum opened in 2008, and more than six million people have visited this museum on Pennsylvania Avenue between the United States Capitol and the White House.

2. **Run-on sentences**

A run-on sentence (also known as a fused sentence) occurs when two independent clauses are crammed together with no punctuation between them, for example,

> The Newseum explores the challenges confronting freedom around the world in a variety of ways its First Amendment Center serves as a forum for the study and debate of free expression issues.

This can easily be fixed, as well:

> The Newseum explores the challenges confronting freedom around the world in a variety of ways; its First Amendment Center serves as a forum for the study and debate of free expression issues.

◀ BRIEF GUIDE TO PUNCTUATION & GRAMMAR ▶

The Newseum explores the challenges confronting freedom around the world in a variety of ways. Its First Amendment Center serves as a forum for the study and debate of free expression issues.

3. **Sentence fragments**

A fragment occurs when you punctuate an incomplete thought as a sentence. Writers create fragments for a variety of reasons, including mistaking long sentences for complete thoughts, failing to have subjects or predicates, and punctuating dependent clauses as sentences without joining them with independent clauses

Missing predicate:

The Newseum's Comcast-sponsored 9/11 Gallery featuring the remains of the broadcast antennae from the very top of the World Trade Center.

This can be fixed by changing "featuring" to "features":

> The Newseum's Comcast-sponsored 9/11 Gallery features the remains of the broadcast antennae from the very top of the World Trade Center.

An independent clause (not a fragment) followed by a dependent clause (a fragment):

> The Newseum is committed to hosting programs to help to generate solutions to some of the most serious national and international challenges of our times. Because the Newseum Institute is dedicated to defending and promoting the freedom guaranteed by the First Amendment to the Constitution as being crucial to protecting our way of life.

The dependent clause may not feel like a fragment because the dependent clause connects very logically to the main clause that precedes it. It just isn't connected correctly grammatically. Some students are very uncomfortable with long sentences, but, if they make sense and are punctuated correctly, there is nothing wrong with them if they are not overdone. Sentence variety is important.

The dependent clause needs to be correctly attached to the main clause:

Because the Newseum Institute is dedicated to defending and promoting the freedom guaranteed by the First Amendment to the Constitution as being crucial to protecting our way of life, it is committed to hosting programs to help to generate solutions to some of the most serious national and international challenges of our times.

Moving the dependent clause before the main clause, adding the required comma before the main clause, and using the pronoun "it" instead of "the Newseum Institute" in the main clause works just fine.

Recognizing and Punctuating Restrictive and Nonrestrictive Elements

Restrictive material is grammatically and logically essential to the sentence it is within. If you remove the material, you change the meaning of the sentence. You do not alter the meaning of a sentence by removing nonrestrictive material. This material may contain important ideas that a writer wishes to convey—the point to remember is that nonrestrictive information is not unimportant information; it is simply information that would not alter the sentence it is in if it wasn't there.

Here is an example (underlined) of a restrictive element in a sentence:

People <u>with extreme confirmation bias</u> cannot critically evaluate information.

If we take the restrictive element out, we have the following:

People cannot critically evaluate information.

The meaning has clearly changed—the altered sentence does not convey the actual intent of the original sentence. In this version, no people at all can critically evaluate information.

Here is an example (underlined) of a nonrestrictive element in a sentence:

Confirmation bias, <u>which is also called confirmatory bias or "my side" bias</u>, is the tendency to look for, favor, and remember information in a way that confirms a person's preexisting beliefs.

If we take the nonrestrictive element out, we have the following, which does not change the sentence's essential meaning:

> Confirmation bias is the tendency to look for, favor, and remember information in a way that confirms a person's preexisting beliefs.

1. **Do not set restrictive elements off with any punctuation marks.** If you look at the following example, you'll see that the restrictive element, which is underlined, is crucial to the meaning of the sentence.

   News sources <u>with high standards of integrity</u> are quite valuable.

If we removed the restrictive element, the sentence would be telling people that all news sources are always valuable.

2. **Set nonrestrictive elements off with commas.** If you look at the following example, you'll see that the nonrestrictive element, which is underlined, is not crucial to the meaning of the sentence.

   Media literacy, <u>a key twenty-first century skill</u>, is an important part of critical thinking and informed analysis.

If we removed the nonrestrictive element, we would not be changing the essential meaning of the sentence:

> Media literacy is an important part of critical thinking and informed analysis.

Other Uses of Commas

1. **When a phrase precedes an independent clause, separate them with a comma.**

Generally, we punctuate phrases in relation to main clauses the same way we punctuate dependent clauses in relation to main clauses.

> Due to confirmation bias, many people recall news in a way that confirms their preexisting beliefs.

When the phrase is very short, and there is no possibility of confusion, the comma is optional.

Every day, Americans are bombarded with information and misinformation.

Every day Americans are bombarded with information and misinformation.

Both sentences are clear. But imagine reading a sentence that begins with this phrase:

> While eating very young children . . .

When you finish the sentence, you realize it wasn't what you initially thought:

> While eating very young children should not be left alone because they might choke.

It would have been clearer to begin with had the writer punctuated it correctly, putting a comma after the introductory phrase to signal the beginning of the dependent clause:

> While eating, very young children should not be left alone because they might choke.

Do not use a comma with phrases following main clauses.

> Very young should children should not be left alone while eating.

2. **Use commas to separate three or more items in a series** (as long as the items themselves don't have commas), including a comma before the word "and" joining the last item to the list. You may have been told by some people to leave the comma before "and" out; however, MLA, the most common style arbiter, requires this comma. Other styles, such as journalistic style, do not include it.

   I'm taking history, English, chemistry, and art history this semester.

Two or more words that are the same parts of speech in a series, like adjectives or adverbs, should be separated from each other with commas (but not the terms that they modify).

The sky was a deep, clear, beautiful blue. (Three adjectives modifying a noun.)

The documentary provided a deeply moving, intellectually challenging experience. (Two adverbs modifying two adjectives).

3. **Use a comma after introductory words—like "stated," "said," "says," "asserts," "suggests," and "writes" when they come before direct quotations.**

Oscar Wilde said, "Selfishness is not living as one wishes to live, it is asking others to live as one wishes to live."

Note: If you follow words like "said" and "stated" with the relative pronoun "that," do not use a comma before the quotation.

Oscar Wilde said that "A thing is not necessarily true because a man dies for it."

4. **Use a comma before and after quoted material that you interrupt with a phrase of your own within a sentence.**

"Think about the way you read as a child," Maria Tatar stated, "there are constant epiphanies."

5. **Use a comma before quotations preceded by introductory phrases.**

To quote Graham Greene, "People who like quotes love meaningless generalizations."

6. **Use a comma before a contrasting element.**
I want the vegetarian pizza, not the pepperoni one.

7. **Use a comma to set off "or" and a word or phrase when they are being offered as a synonym or definition of a word preceding these.**

He cooked the dish with onions and chickpeas, or garbanzo beans, as we call them.

It was a *beau geste*, or "beautiful gesture."

8. **Use commas to set cities off from states and regions, states and regions off from countries, days.**

Using Semicolons

1. **Use semicolons to set off two closely related independent clauses when they don't have a coordinating conjunction between them.**

   Oklahoma averaged about two earthquakes greater than or equal to magnitude 2.7 per year between 1980 and 2000; this number jumped to about 2,500 in 2014 and 4,000 in 2015.

   Oklahoma doesn't normally get large earthquakes; however, the state's risk is now equal to that of California.

   Three million Americans are at risk from human-induced earthquakes caused by a process in fracking; Oklahoma had fewer earthquakes in 2016 than in 2015, however, due to restrictions on fracking.

2. **Use semicolons to set off items in a series of three or more when one or more of those items has a comma.**

The following series names three cities:

   His journeys have included visits to Quito, Ecuador; Rome, Italy; and Athens, Greece.

Sometimes people get confused and reverse the semicolon and commas. Remember that in situations like those above, the commas are serving as connectors—they connect an explanation, description, or some other piece of information about an item to that item—and the semicolons are functioning as separators between different items. Ask yourself this question: "Which looks bigger and stronger, the comma [,] or the semicolon [;]?" Make sure that you understand where each item begins and leaves off, and put the semicolons where you are separating these items.

   His journeys have included visits to [1] Quito, Ecuador; [2] Rome, Italy; and [3] Athens, Greece.

◀ BRIEF GUIDE TO PUNCTUATION & GRAMMAR ▶

In MLA format, we put a comma in front of "and" when it sets off the last item in a series of three or more. When the items themselves have commas, turn all the commas that we would ordinarily have in a series into semicolons, including the one preceding "and."

Using Colons

1. **Colons are used to introduce sentence elements, but only after independent clauses.** Use them when an independent clause is designed to create a feeling of anticipation for the information that is to follow. They can introduce a series, direct quotations, or even other independent clauses if the second clause interprets, explains, or amplifies the first.

   Authors who have used classic fairy tales as the basis of fiction and poetry include the following: Angela Carter, Margaret Atwood, and Anne Sexton.

   Polonius gave this advice to Laertes: "Neither a borrower nor a lender be."

Do not use a colon if the element being introduced does not follow an independent clause. (Hint: you won't have a colon after a verb.)

   Authors who have used classic fairy tales as the basis of fiction and poetry include Angela Carter, Margaret Atwood, and Anne Sexton.

2. **Colons are used between titles and subtitles.**

   The True Believer: Thoughts on the Nature of Mass Movements

Note: An exception occurs when a title is followed by another punctuation mark before the subtitle, as in the following example:

   Trust Us, We're Experts! How Industry Manipulates Science and Gambles with Your Future

Using Apostrophes

The apostrophe has two primary uses: forming contractions and making nouns possessive. In the past, it was commonly used to make numerals denoting decades and years plural, but MLA style no longer recommends this: you should write "the 1990s," not "the 1990's," though you would write "the '90s" since that is a contraction.

1. **Use the apostrophe to form contractions by inserting it in place of missing letters or numbers.**

    "It's" is the contraction of "it is" (it is not the possessive form of "it").

2. **Use the apostrophe to make nouns—not pronouns—possessive. Where or whether an "s" is added depends on whether a word is singular or plural and on its spelling.**

When words do not end with an "s," make them possessive by adding an apostrophe and then an "s."

> One <u>cat</u>'s kittens   the <u>children</u>'s toys   the <u>women</u>'s team

When words end with an "s," add only an apostrophe when no extra "s" sound is pronounced.

> two <u>cats</u>' kittens   both <u>houses</u>' roofs   all the <u>bosses</u>' offices

When words end with an "s" or an "s" sound, and an extra "s" sound is added when the word is made possessive, add an apostrophe and an "s" after it.

> her <u>house</u>'s roof   his <u>boss</u>'s office   the <u>fox</u>'s lair

Subjects in sentences may share possession of something or have separate possession of different things.

With shared possession—when the subjects are functioning as a single unit—add the apostrophe and, if necessary, an additional "s" after the last name or item in the series.

> Amal and Ayda's home is near the college.

If the subjects do not share possession, make each name or item in the series possessive.

> Michaela's and Angel's homes are several miles apart.

Using Quotation Marks

1. **Quotation marks are used when you use someone else's exact phrasing** (unless the quotation is over four lines in your paper, in which case you indent two tabs (one inch) from the left margin instead).

   > Emilio said, "I love the novels and short stories of Neil Gaiman."

2. **Quotation marks are used around the titles of works like poems, short stories, essays, and articles** (works that are contained in periodicals and books).

   > Neil Gaiman's "Snow, Glass Apples" is based on the classic fairy tale "Snow White."

For quotations or titles of such works inside a quotation, use single quotation marks (also called "inverted commas") inside the quotation. Use the apostrophe key on your keyboard.

> Emilio said, "My favorite short story is Neil Gaiman's 'Snow, Glass Apples.'"

Putting periods and commas outside of closing quotation marks is not correct in MLA, APA, or other standard American formats. The only time you should have a sentence's period outside a closing quotation mark is when the sentence is followed by a parenthetical in-text citation. The period follows the citation unless you have an indented quotation. If you need a colon or a semicolon after material in quotation marks, the colon or semicolon should follow the closing quotation mark.

> Aliyah analyzed a standard fairy tale motif in "The Courtship of Mr. Lyon": transformation.

> Tomas wrote about "The Tiger's Bride"; it is the second Angela Carter short story based on the fairy tale "Beauty and the Beast."

If you directly quote a question or if a question mark is part of a title, the question mark goes inside the closing quotation mark. Also, only one terminal punctuation mark is used with quotation marks, so you don't follow a quotation with a period if you have a quotation mark inside.

> "She asked, "What was the name of that story we read by Joyce Carol Oates?"
>
> The name of the story is "Where Are You Going, Where Have You Been?"

If you ask a question about material enclosed within quotation marks, the question mark goes outside the closing quotation mark.

> Did you know that Alejandro G. Iñárritu's movie Birdman includes a fictional Broadway play based on the Raymond Carver story "What We Talk about When We Talk about Love"?

Using Terminal Punctuation Marks

Periods, question marks, and exclamation points are all called terminal punctuation marks because they all terminate sentences. Do not confuse the decimal point with the period. They look exactly alike and both are made using the period key, but decimals are used with numbers, such as fractions. Do not put a space after a decimal point. Always follow periods with spaces. The Modern Language Association now recommends using only one space after periods, not two.

Using Question Marks

Use question marks at the end of sentences that ask questions, including rhetorical questions and requests made in the form of questions. A rhetorical question is a question asked with no expectation of an answer. The question might be one that has an obvious answer, but it has been asked to make a point, to persuade, or for literary effect (thus the term "rhetorical question").

> What topic did you choose for your paper? Are you crazy?

Remember that placement of question marks in relation to quotation marks is important. If you are quoting a question, put the closing quotation mark after the question mark.

> The professor asked, "Does anyone have any questions?"

If you are asking a question about a quotation, place the question mark after the closing quotation mark.

> Did you really mean it when you said, "You're fired"?

Using Ellipsis Marks

Ellipsis marks (a set is called an ellipsis) are indicated by three periods. An ellipsis can appear next to other punctuation, including a sentence's period (resulting in four periods). Use four only when the words one or both sides of the ellipsis make full sentences. The MLA recommends that you have spaces before and after each ellipsis mark

1. **Ellipses are used to indicate the omission of quoted material.**

The current convention is to put brackets around ellipses that you insert into direct quotations to make it clear that the ellipses aren't part of the original passage.

> "In our time, political speech and writing are largely the defense of the indefensible [. . . .] Thus political language has to consist largely of euphemism" (Orwell 113).

The use of brackets around ellipses within quoted material is a relatively recent practice, so you have probably seen more examples of ellipses without brackets than with them. The brackets indicate that the writer quoting George Orwell added the ellipses, not Orwell.

2. **Ellipses are used to indicate a sentence or clause that is allowed to deliberately trail off, suggesting a pause or unfinished comment or idea.**

> Juana was assured that the used car she was thinking of buying was very reliable, however . . . .

◀ PART SIX ▶

Using Brackets

We use square brackets when we insert material into, delete, or change material within quotations in order to make our additions or changes clearly distinct from the actual quoted material.

1. **Use brackets to add explanatory information to a direct quotation.**

   Noam Chomsky said, "If you don't have [an idea what you're looking for], exploring the Internet is just picking out random factoids that don't mean anything."

2. **Use brackets when you change an upper-case letter to a lower-case letter or a lower-case letter to an upper-case letter in a direct quotation.**

   Here are some lines from Theodore Roethke's poem "The Waking":

   Great Nature has another thing to do
   To you and me, so take the lively air

   If you wished to incorporate these lines into a sentence of your own and still follow conventional capitalization guidelines for sentences, you could write the following:

   I feel, like Roethke, that "Great Nature has another thing to do // [to] you and me,"

   Note: A forward slash is used to indicate a division between lines of poetry in the original version, but it does not need to be enclosed in brackets. If a stanza break occurs, indicate that with two forward slashes.

3. **Use brackets when you change a word in a quotation.**

   Take, for example, the following sentence from an article by Matthew Gilbert: "His voices, and the voices in his dramatic monologues, are unrelentingly curious and honest." Out of context, this could be a bit confusing, so it could be altered to the following:

   "[Bidart's] voices, and the voices in his dramatic monologues, are unrelentingly curious and honest."

4. **Use brackets around the term sic (Latin for "thus") to indicate errors or unusual spelling variations that are "thus in the original."**

   Jonson told Drummond that "Shakspeer [sic] wanted art."

Sic is Latin, and the MLA suggests italicizing foreign words.

5. **Use brackets around ellipses [. . .] when following MLA style to indicate that material that has been deleted** (only delete words if you are in no way altering the meaning of the original passage).

   With the arrival of peace in Europe in 1815 [. . . .] There was a new emphasis on technology and applied science."

In the example above, the entire end of the sentence was cut. If words within a single sentence were cut, there would be only three ellipses and the word following the bracket would not be capitalized unless it was a proper noun.

PART SEVEN

PRACTICE EXERCISES AND KEYS

The following pages contain exercises to help you practice the key elements of MLA documentation layout, parenthetical citations, and works cited pages.

MLA WORKS CITED PRACTICE EXERCISES AND KEYS

Titles of books, articles, films, etc. and the names of periodicals, websites, and databases are all in bold to make them easier to identify. Also, most are titles are in all lowercase letters, so they need to be capitalized correctly.

Works Cited Exercise #1: A Book by One Author

Create a Work Cited page for the following book. The book is titled **the poisoned well: empire and its legacy in the middle east**. Oxford University Press published it in 2016. Its author is Roger Hardy.

Works Cited Exercise #2: Two Books by One Author

Create a Work Cited page for two books by author Naomi Klein. One book is titled **no logo: taking aim at the brand bullies**, which was published by Alfred A. Knopf, Inc. It was published in 1999. The other book is titled **this changes everything: capitalism vs. the climate**, which was published by Simon and Schuster, Incorporated. It was published in 2014.

Works Cited Exercise #3: Two Books by Two Authors

Create a Work Cited page for the following books. One book is titled **toxic sludge is good for you: lies, damn lies and the public relations industry**. Common Courage Press published it in 1995. Its authors are John Stauber and Sheldon Rampton. The other book is titled **trust us, we're experts! how industry manipulates science and gambles with your future**. Penguin Putnam published it in 2001. Its authors are Sheldon Rampton and John Stauber (note the order).

Works Cited Exercise #4: One Book by Four Authors

Create a Work Cited page for the following book: **introduction to psychology**. Cengage Learning published it in 2014. Its authors are Susan Nolen-Hoeksema, Barbara L. Fredrickson, Geoffrey R. Loftus, and Christel Lutz.

Works Cited Exercise #5: eBook and Kindle Book

The eBook is called **critical thinking and higher order thinking: a current perspective**. The information in the database is given exactly as follows: "By: Shaughnessy, Michael F. Hauppauge, NY : Nova Science Publishers, Inc. 2012. eBook." It is in the Bakersfield College eBook Collection. The URL follows: http://ezproxy.bakersfieldcollege.edu:2105/ehost/detail. (This is not the entire URL, which was quite long—we'll just pretend it is.)

The Kindle book is titled **parable of the sower** It is by Octavia E. Butler. The publisher's name is Open Road Media Sci-Fi & Fantasy, and it was published in 2012

Works Cited Exercise #6: One Work from an Anthology

Create a Work Cited page for a story in an anthology titled **an introduction to literature**. The editors of the anthology are William Burto and Sylvan Barnet. Alfred A. Knopf, Inc., published it in 2002. The story is titled **fleur**. It is by Louise Erdrich. It is on pages 460 to 469.

Works Cited Exercise #7: Multiple Works from the Same Anthology

Create a Work Cited page for two articles from an anthology titled **navigating america: information competency and research for the twenty-first century**.

The work by Kyle Bishop is titled **raising the dead: unearthing the nonliterary origins of zombie cinema**. It is on pages 463 to 476. The work by Jacqueline Bach is titled from **nerds to napoleans**. It is on pages 437 to 449.

◀ MLA WORKS CITED PRACTICE EXERCISES AND KEYS ▶

The editors of **navigating america: information competency and research for the twenty-first century** are David Moton and Gloria Dumler. The publisher is McGraw-Hill Higher Education. It was published in 2010.

WORKS CITED EXERCISE #8: TWO WORKS FROM THE SAME ANTHOLOGY AND ONE WORK FROM A SEPARATE ANTHOLOGY.

Create a Work Cited page for three short stories.

Two are in an anthology called **literature: a portable anthology**. It is edited by Janet E. Gardner, Beverly Lawn, Jack Ridl, and Peter Schakel. It was published by Bedford/St. Martin's in 2012. The stories are **the lesson** by Toni Cade Bambara on pages 330 to 336, and **cathedral** by Raymond Carver on pages 299 to 311.

The third is in an anthology called science fiction: the science fiction research anthology. The editors are Patrick S. Warrick, Charles G. Waugh, and Martin H. Greenberg. It was published by HarperCollins Publishers, Inc., in 1988. The story is titled when it changed. It is by Joanna Russ, and it is on pages 411 to 416.

WORKS CITED EXERCISE #9: TWO WORKS FROM SCHOLARLY JOURNALS: PRINT AND DATABASE.

Create a Work Cited page for two articles from scholarly (academic) journals, one from a print version and one from a database.

The print article is called **with facebook, blogs, and fake news, teens reject journalistic "objectivity."** Its author is Regina Marchi. The **journal's name is journal of communication inquiry**. The journal's volume number is 36 and its issue number is 3. It was published In July 2012, and the article is on pages 246 to 262.

The database article is **advancing racism with facebook: frequency and purpose of facebook use and acceptance of prejudiced and egalitarian messages** by Shannon M. Rauch and Kimberley Schanz. The journal is **com-**

puters in human behavior. The publication information is given as follows: "May2013, Vol. 29 Issue 3, p610-615. 6p." The database is **academic search premier**. The DOI is doi:10.1016/j.chb.2012.11.011.

WORKS CITED EXERCISE #10: TWO WORKS FROM SCHOLARLY JOURNALS: DATABASE AND ONLINE-ONLY

The journal in the database **academic search premier** is **journal of american culture**. The article is **blood ties: the vampire lover in the popular romance**. Publication information is presented as follows: "By: Bailie, Helen T. Jun2011, Vol. 34 Issue 2, p141-148. 8p. DOI: 10.1111/j.1542-734X.2011.00770.x."

The online-only journal is slayage: the journal of whedon studies. It is by Franklin D. Worrell; it is titled negotiations after hegemony: buffy and gender. It is in volume 14, issue 2, in the summer 2016 issue. The URL is http://www.whedonstudies.tv/uploads/2/6/2/8/26288593/worrell_slayage_14.2.pdf.

WORKS CITED EXERCISE #11: THREE WORKS FROM MAGAZINES: PRINT, DATABASE, AND ONLINE

The work from a print magazine is **werewolves in sheep's clothing**. It is by Michael Coney, and the magazine is named **fantasy & science fiction**. It was published in the September 1996 issue. The magazine's cover says that it is Vol. 91, Issue 3. The work is on pages 130 to 161.

The magazine article from a database is **werewolves in their youth**. The database is **academic search premier**. The magazine is **the new yorker**. The database presents publication information as follows: "3/29/93, Vol. 69 Issue 6, p78. 10p." The URL is http://ezproxy.bakersfieldcollege.edu: 2053/ehost/detail/. (This is not the entire URL—we'll just pretend that it is.)

The magazine article from an online magazine is **how american werewolf in london transformed horror-comedy**. (Note: **american werewolf in london** is a film.) It is by Joshua Rothkopf. It is in the August 19, 2016 issue

◀ MLA WORKS CITED PRACTICE EXERCISES AND KEYS ▶

of **rolling stone**. The URL is http://www.rollingstone.com/movies/news/how-american-werewolf-in-london-transformed-horror-comedy-w434829.

WORKS CITED EXERCISE #12: THREE WORKS FROM NEWSPAPERS: PRINT, DATABASE, AND ONLINE

The print article is called **refugees hear a foreign word: welcome**. It is by Jodi Kantor and Catrin Einhorn. It is in **the new york times**. It was in the 7/1/2016 issue, and it begins on page 1 and is continued later in the paper.

The article in the database **newspaper source plus is district officials favor accepting syrian refugees**. The database presents information as follows: "By: Brown, Stacy M. 11/26/2015, Vol. 51 Issue 7, p1-8. 2p." The newspaper is **washington informer**. "P1-8. 2p" indicates that it begins on page 1 and then skips to page 8. The URL is http://ezproxy.bakersfieldcollege.edu:2105/ehost/detail/. (Sort of.)

The online article is by Raja Abdulrahim in **the wall street journal**. The article is **aleppo's hospitals shut down after heavy bombardment**. It was posted November 19, 2016 02:45 p.m. The URL is http://www.wsj.com/articles/aleppos-hospitals-shut-down-after-heavy-bombardment-1479549512?tesla=y.

WORKS CITED EXERCISE #13: ARTICLES ON WEBSITES

Create a works cited page for three articles found on websites.

The sponsoring government agency is Centers for Disease Control and Prevention. That is also the name of the site. The article is titled **vaccines do not cause autism**. The URL is https://www.cdc.gov/vaccinesafety/concerns/autism.html. No author is given. The page was last updated on November 23, 2015.

The sponsoring NGO is Doctors without Borders. That is also the name of the site. The article is titled **east aleppo: a ceasefire fails, shelling resumes, and hope fades**. The URL is http://www.doctorswithoutborders.org/article/east-aleppo-ceasefire-fails-shelling-resumes-and-hope-fades. It was posted on December 14, 2016.

◀ PART SEVEN ▶

The sponsoring NGO is Union of Concerned Scientists. That is also the name of the site. The article is titled **the us military on the front lines of rising seas (2016)**. The URL is http://www.ucsusa.org/global-warming/global-warming-impacts/sea-level-rise-flooding-us-military-bases#.WJU6RxiZM9U. The authors are Erika Spanger-Siegfried, Kristina Dahl, Astrid Caldas, and Shana. No date is given.

WORKS CITED EXERCISE #14: A FEATURE FILM AND A DOCUMENTARY

Create a Works Cited page for the following two movies: **going clear: scientology and the prison of belief** is a 2015 documentary film directed by Alex Gibney. The company is Jigsaw Productions. For this exercise, focus on the film. **The master** is a 2012 film written and directed by Paul Thomas Anderson and starring Joaquin Phoenix, Philip Seymour Hoffman, and Amy Adams. The company is JoAnne Sellar Productions. For this exercise, focus on Anderson.

WORKS CITED EXERCISE #15: A YOUTUBE VIDEO AND A SERIES ON NETFLIX

The series **black mirror**, which was produced by House of Tomorrow and shown on Netflix in 2016. It was created by Charlie Brooker. Your focus is the series.

The video is titled **BLC theatre presents hamlet by william shakespeare**. (Note that **hamlet** is the title of a play.) It was uploaded August 20, 2013, by BLA Productions. It is directed by Peter Bloedel. For this exercise, your focus is the video. The URL is https://www.youtube.com/watch?v=zz6GL6AFphU.

◀ KEYS TO THE EXERCISES ▶

KEYS TO THE EXERCISES

WORKS CITED EXERCISE #1 KEY: A BOOK BY ONE AUTHOR

Work Cited

Hardy, Roger. *The Poisoned Well: Empire and Its Legacy in the Middle East.* Oxford UP, 2016.

All works cited entries with authors begin the same way: with the name of the author, last name first (if there are other authors, do not reverse their first and last names). Follow with a period. Follow with the title of the book in italics, also followed by a period. Always include subtitles if provided. Don't look at the cover or spine of a page to determine a subtitle because it may be left out. Look at the title page and the publication data. Precede subtitles with colons unless the title ends with an exclamation point or question mark. Follow with the publisher's full name, except for "business" words and abbreviations like "Inc.," and a comma. Follow with the year and a period. Capitalize all words in titles except the following (unless they are the first or last words of a title or subtitle): articles ("a," "an," and "the"), prepositions ("of," "with," "above," "in," "over," "before," "at," etc.), coordinating conjunctions ("for," "and," "nor," "but," "or," "yet," "so"), and the "to" in infinitives (as in "How to Capitalize Titles").

WORKS CITED EXERCISE #2 KEY: TWO BOOKS BY ONE AUTHOR

Works Cited

Klein, Naomi. *No Logo: Taking Aim at the Brand Bullies.* Alfred A. Knopf, 1999.

---. *This Changes Everything: Capitalism vs. the Climate.* Simon and Schuster, 2014.

All entries with authors begin the same way: with the author's, first (or only) author's last name first and a period. Follow with the book in italics and a period. Include subtitles if provided. Precede subtitles with colons unless the title ends with an exclamation point or question mark. Follow with the publisher's full name, except for "business" words and abbreviations like "Inc.," and a comma. Follow with the year and a period. Capitalize all words in titles except the following (unless they are the first or last words of a title or subtitle): articles ("a," "an," and "the"), prepositions ("of," "with," "above," "in," "over," "before," "at," etc.), coordinating conjunctions ("for," "and," "nor," "but," "or," "yet," "so"), and the "to" in infinitives. When you have the same author for more than one source, use three hyphens instead of the name for every entry after the first one by that author. Always arrange entries in alphabetical order. Since we had the same author, we look to the first important word of the title (we ignore "a," "an," and "the" if they begin a title) to determine order. "N" comes before "T."

WORKS CITED EXERCISE #3 KEY: TWO BOOKS BY TWO AUTHORS

Works Cited

Rampton, Sheldon, and John Stauber. *Trust Us, We're Experts! How Industry Manipulates Science and Gambles with Your Future.* Penguin Putnam, 2001.

Stauber, John, and Sheldon Rampton. *Toxic Sludge Is Good for You: Lies, Damn Lies and the Public Relations Industry.* Common Courage Press, 1995.

All works cited entries with authors begin the same way: with the name of the author, last name first (if there are other authors, do not reverse their first and last names) With two authors, follow the first author's name with a comma. This is the only time in MLA or other format styles that you separate a series of only two items with a comma, and we only do this for the names of people at the beginning of works cited entries. Follow with a period. Do not change the order of the authors as they are presented; the order is important, as it usually indicates the leader of a project, the major contributor, or the winner of a coin flip. Follow with the title of the book in italics, also followed by a

◀ KEYS TO THE EXERCISES ▶

period. Always include subtitles if provided. Precede subtitles with colons unless the title ends with an exclamation point or question mark. Follow with the publisher's full name, except for "business" words and abbreviations like "Inc.," and a comma. Follow with the year and a period. Capitalize all words in titles except the following: articles, prepositions, coordinating conjunctions, and the "to" in infinitives unless they are the first or last words of a title or subtitle. Do not use three hyphens instead of the names of multiple authors for an entry unless the names are presented in exactly the same order. Since the order of the authors (even though they are the same people) is different for each of the two books, we do not use the three hyphens to replace their names in the entry for *Toxic Sludge is Good for You: Lies, Damn Lies and the Public Relations Industry*.

WORKS CITED EXERCISE #4 KEY: ONE BOOK BY FOUR AUTHORS

Work Cited

Nolen-Hoeksema, Susan, et al. *Introduction to Psychology*. Cengage Learning, 2014.

All works cited entries with authors begin the same way: with the name of the author, last name first (if there are other authors, do not reverse their first and last names). With three or more authors, follow the first author's name with a comma and et al. Follow with a period. Follow with the title of the book in italics, also followed by a period. Follow with the publisher's full name, except for "business" words and abbreviations like "Inc.," and a comma. Follow with the year and a period. Capitalize all words in titles except the following: articles, prepositions, coordinating conjunctions, and the "to" in infinitives unless they are the first or last words of a title or subtitle.

If your professor wished you to list all the names (which is not the MLA's preference, but is allowed), the entry would look like this.

Nolen-Hoeksema, Susan, Barbara L. Fredrickson, Geoffrey R. Loftus, and Christel Lutz. *Introduction to Psychology*. Cengage Learning, 2014.

Works Cited Exercise #5 Key: Ebook And Kindle Book

Shaughnessy, Michael F. *Critical Thinking and Higher Order Thinking: A Current Perspective*. Nova Science Publishers, 2012. Bakersfield College eBook Collection, ezproxy.bakersfieldcollege.edu:2105/ehost/detail.

We follow the year with a period since that is the last component of the first "container." The first component of the second "container" is the title of the container, in this case the BC collection. The URL is its "location." You should break the URL to move part of it to the next line. Remember to drop "http//" from the beginning of the URL. Remember that databases often give you publication information that you don't need in an entry, such as city of publication. Capitalize all words in titles except the following: articles, prepositions, coordinating conjunctions, and the "to" in infinitives unless they are the first or last words of a title or subtitle.

Butler, Octavia E. *Parable of the Sower*. Open Road Media Sci-Fi & Fantasy, 2012. Kindle.

This entry is exactly like the entry for the print version of a book, except that it includes a second "container" that follows the date of publication. The title of the second "container" is Kindle.

Works Cited Exercise #6 Key: One Work From An Anthology

Work Cited

Erdrich, Louise. "Fleur." *An Introduction to Literature*, edited by William Burto and Sylvan Barnet, Alfred K. Knopf, 2002, pp. 460-69.

When you have only one work from an anthology, all the information for the anthology and the work go in one entry. Begin with the author of the work, first and last names reversed, and a period. Follow with the title of the short

◀ KEYS TO THE EXERCISES ▶

story, article, poem, or essay in quotation marks and a period. Periods go inside closing quotation marks. (If an entire play or novel is contained in the anthology, italicize it.) Follow with the title of the anthology in italics. Capitalize all words in titles except the following: articles, prepositions, coordinating conjunctions, and the "to" in infinitives unless they are the first or last words of a title or subtitle. Follow the anthology with a comma, "edited by," and the editors' names. Since we are not utilizing them to put anything into alphabetical order, do not reverse the first and last names of any of the editors. Do not follow the first editor's name with a comma. Follow the last editor's name with a comma, the publisher's full name (omitting business words or abbreviations), a comma, the year, a comma, and the first and last page numbers, preceded by "pp." Drop the first numeral of the last page number if it is within the same range of a hundred as the first page. End, as always, with a period.

WORKS CITED EXERCISE #7 KEY: TWO WORKS FROM THE SAME ANTHOLOGY

Works Cited

Bach, Jacqueline. "From Nerds to Napoleons." Moton and Dumler, pp. 437-49.

Bishop, Kyle. "Raising the Dead: Unearthing the Nonliterary Origins of Zombie Cinema." Moton and Dumler, pp. 463-76.

Moton, David, and Gloria Dumler, editors. *Navigating America: Information Competency and Research for the Twenty-First Century*. McGraw-Hill Higher Education, 2010.

To avoid unnecessary repetition of publishing information, when you have more than one work from an anthology, provide one entry just for the anthology and provide separate cross-references for each of the works that you take from it. The anthology has all the regular components of a book, with the addition of the abbreviation for "editors" after the editors' names. There are two editors, but we only reverse the first and last names of the first editor. Note that a comma precedes "and" even though there are only two editors in this list. (In sentences, we do not use commas before "and" with a series of only two items.) Leave people in the order they are in a work—don't change the order to put them into alphabetical order. If there had been three or more editors, you could replace the names of everyone after the first with "et al."

A typical cross-reference has only four elements: (1) the author of the work, (2) the title of the work, (3) the editors' last names, and (4) the page numbers of the work, preceded by "pp." Each entry is separate. As always, arrange the entries alphabetically by the authors' last names. The first line of each entry should be flush with the left margin. Do not combine the two stories into one entry or group them under the anthology. They will follow their anthology only if alphabetical order determines it.

Capitalize all words in titles except the following: articles, prepositions, coordinating conjunctions, and the "to" in infinitives unless they are the first or last words of a title or subtitle. As the example indicates, you also capitalize the word following a hyphen in a compound word.

WORKS CITED EXERCISE #8 KEY: TWO WORKS FROM THE SAME ANTHOLOGY AND ONE WORK FROM A SEPARATE ANTHOLOGY.

Works Cited

Bambara, Toni Cade. "The Lesson." Gardner, et al. pp. 330-36.

Carver, Raymond. "Cathedral." Gardner, et al. pp. 299-311.

Gardner, Janet E., et al, editors. *Literature: A Portable Anthology*. Bedford/St. Martin's, 2012.

Russ, Joanna. "When It Changed." *Science Fiction: The Science Fiction Research Anthology*, edited by Patrick S. Warrick, et al., HarperCollins, 1988, pp. 411-16.

◀ KEYS TO THE EXERCISES ▶

As always, arrange the entries alphabetically by authors' and editors' (if they are the first in an entry) last names. Each entry is separate. The first line of each entry should be flush with the left margin. Do not combine the two stories from one anthology into one entry or group them under the anthology. They will follow their anthology only if alphabetical order coincidentally determines it. Remember, as this key shows, that we treat single and multiple entries from anthologies differently. See the more detailed explanations in earlier keys. Capitalize all words in titles except the following: articles, prepositions, coordinating conjunctions, and the "to" in infinitives unless they are the first or last words of a title or subtitle.

WORKS CITED EXERCISE #9 KEY: TWO WORKS FROM SCHOLARLY JOURNALS: PRINT AND DATABASE.

Works Cited

Marchi, Regin. "With Facebook, Blogs, and Fake News, Teens Reject Journalistic Objectivity.'" *Journal of Communication Inquiry*, vol. 36, no. 3, July 2012, pp. 246-62.

Rauch, Shannon M., and Kimberley Schanz. "Advancing Racism with Facebook: Frequency and Purpose of Facebook Use and Acceptance of Prejudiced and Egalitarian Messages." *Computers in Human Behavior*, vol. 29, no. 3, May 2013, pp. 610-15. *Academic Search Premier*, doi:10.1016/j.chb.2012.11.011.

Entries for articles begin as all entries do, with the author's name, first and last names reversed. When there is more than one author, only reverse the first and last names of the first author, and do not change the order of the authors as they are presented. With two authors, follow the second name with a comma. Follow with a period. Give the title of the article in quotation marks, with a period inside the closing quotation mark. Capitalize all words in titles except the following: articles, prepositions, coordinating conjunctions, and the "to" in infinitives unless they are the first or last words of a title or subtitle. Commas follow all other elements in the "container," except the last element. The next element is the journal, which should be italicized. It is followed by the volume number, which is preceded by "vol."; note that we do not capitalize either "vol." or "no." Follow with the issue number; note that we use "no.," not "Issue." Follow with the month or season (do not add a comma after it), the year, and the page numbers. (Had there been only one-page number, we would use "p." not "pp."). Note: "The preposition "with" is capitalized in the first entry because it is the first word in the title. All other prepositions and coordinating conjunctions in both titles are lower case.

The article from the database is treated exactly the same way the print article is, except that we move to a second "container." The page numbers are the "location" and last element in the first "container," so they are followed by a period. Remember that databases often give you publication information that you don't need in an entry, such as "6p," the number of pages. Just the first and last page numbers are needed, and drop the first numeral in the last page number since it is in the same range of a hundred as the first page number. The title of the second "container" is the database, and the "location" is the Digital Object Identifier (DOI).

WORKS CITED EXERCISE #10 KEY: TWO WORKS FROM SCHOLARLY JOURNALS: DATABASE AND ONLINE-ONLY

Works Cited

Bailie, Helen T. "Blood Ties: The Vampire Lover in the Popular Romance." *Journal of American Culture*, vol. 32, no, 2, June 2011, pp. 141-48. *Academic Search Premier,* doi10.1111/j.1542-734X.2011.00770.x.

Worrell, Franklin D. "Negotiations after Hegemony: Buffy and Gender." *Slayage: The Journal of Whedon Studies*, vol. 14, no. 2, Summer 2016, www.whedonstudies.tv/uploads/2/6/2/8/26288593/worrell_slayage_14.2.pdf.

◀ KEYS TO THE EXERCISES ▶

Typically, the end of the first "container" for a journal article would be its page numbers; they would be the "location" in the first container. Since this journal does not use page numbers, the Universal Resource Locater (URL) is the "location," which is why it follows the year and a comma, not a period. Drop "http://" MLA format no longer uses abbreviations like "n.p." when page numbers are not provided. If your professor prefers you not to use URLs (they can be quite lengthy), the entry could be formatted as follows:

Worrell, Franklin D. "Negotiations after Hegemony: Buffy and Gender." *Slayage: The Journal of Whedon Studies*, vol. 14, no. 2, Summer 2016, web.

WORKS CITED EXERCISE #11 KEY: THREE WORKS FROM MAGAZINES: PRINT, DATABASE, AND ONLINE

Works Cited

Coney, Michael. "Werewolves in Sheep's Clothing." *Fantasy and Science Fiction*, Sept. 1996, pp. 130-61.

Rothkopf, Joshua. "How *American Werewolf in London* Transformed Horror-Comedy." *Rolling Stone*, 19 Aug. 2016, www.rollingstone.com/movies/news/how-american-werewolf-in-london-transformed-horror-comedy-w434829.

"Werewolves in Their Youth." *The New Yorker*, 29 May 1993, pp. 78-88. *Academic Search Premier*, ezproxy.bakersfieldcollege.edu: 2053/ehost/detail/.

Notes for the first entry: Although the magazine's cover says that it is Vol. 91, Issue 3, we do not supply volumes and issue numbers for magazines. As with databases, sources often give us information that we do not use in works cited entries. Remember to abbreviate all months over four letters, using standard abbreviations.

Notes for the second entry: We have a film title inside the article's title, so we italicize the film. We do not have page numbers, so the end of the first "container"—the "location—is the URL. Your professor may prefer you to substitute the word "web."

Notes for the third entry: Since we do not have an author, begin with the title. (In the body of a paper, you would put the entire noun phrase in the in-text citation, not forgetting the quotation marks [if the noun phrase began with an article, we would drop that]). The database included the volume and issue, but we do not use these for magazines. In the past, we would not use "The" as part of the title for the magazine. We were not told the last page number, but we can do the math: 78 + 10 = 88. Don't forget to drop "http://." For this exercise, we did not provide the entire URL—you would have to type a mind-boggling number of numbers, letters, and symbols. However, in a real paper, you would have to provide the full URL (omitting "https://") Your professor might prefer you to use the name of the company supplying the database, as follows:

"Werewolves in Their Youth." *The New Yorker*, 29 May 1993, pp. 78-88. *Academic Search Premier*, EBSCOhost.

WORKS CITED EXERCISE #12 KEY: THREE WORKS FROM NEWSPAPERS: PRINT, DATABASE, AND ONLINE

Works Cited

Abdulrahim, Raja. "Aleppo's Hospitals Shut Down after Heavy Bombardment." *The Wall Street Journal*, 19 Nov. 2016, 2:45 p.m., www.wsj.com/articles/aleppos-hospitals-shut-down-after-heavy-bombardment-1479549512?tesla=y.

Brown, Stacy M. "District Officials Favor Accepting Syrian Refugees." *Washington Informer*, 26 Nov. 2015, pp. 1+.

◀ KEYS TO THE EXERCISES ▶

Kantor, Jodi, and Catrin Einhorn. "Refugees Hear a Foreign Word: Welcome." *The New York Times*, 1 July 2016, pp. 1+. Newspaper Source Plus, ezproxy.bakersfieldcollege.edu:2105/ehost/detail/.

As always, begin with authors when provided, and follow with the titles of the articles in quotation marks. Capitalize all words in titles except the following: articles, prepositions, coordinating conjunctions, and the "to" in infinitives unless they are the first or last words of a title or subtitle. Follow with the periodical's name in italics; follow with the date of publication (including time, when given), and follow with the "location." For print sources or paginated electronic sources, that means page numbers; if there are no page numbers, as with the article in The Wall Street Journal, that means the URL (without "http:/"). Pay attention to where periods or commas are required.

Alternatives (depending on instructor's preference):

Works Cited

Abdulrahim, Raja. "Aleppo's Hospitals Shut Down after Heavy Bombardment." *The Wall Street Journal*, 19 Nov. 2016, 2:45 p.m., web.

Brown, Stacy M. "District Officials Favor Accepting Syrian Refugees." *Washington Informer*, pp. 1+

Kantor, Jodi, and Catrin Einhorn. "Refugees Hear a Foreign Word: Welcome." *The New York Times*, 1 July 2016, pp. 1+. *Newspaper Source Plus*, EBSCOhost.

Works Cited

"East Aleppo: A Ceasefire Fails, Shelling Resumes, and Hope Fades." *Doctors without Borders*, 14 Dec. 2016, www.doctorswithoutborders.org/article/east-aleppo-ceasefire-fails-shelling-resumes-and-hope-fades.

Spanger-Siegfried, Erika, Kristina Dahl, Astrid Caldas, and Shana Udvardy. "The US Military on the Front Lines of Rising Seas (2016)." *Union of Concerned Scientists*, www.ucsusa.org/global-warming/global- warming-impacts/sea-level-rise-flooding-us-military-bases#.WJU6RxiZM9U.

"Vaccines Do Not Cause Autism." *Centers for Disease Control and Prevention*, 23 Nov. 2015, www.cdc.gov/vaccinesafety/concerns/autism.html.

WORKS CITED EXERCISE #13 KEY: ARTICLES ON WEBSITES

Works Cited

"East Aleppo: A Ceasefire Fails, Shelling Resumes, and Hope Fades." *Doctors without Borders*, 14 Dec. 2016, www.doctorswithoutborders.org/article/east-aleppo-ceasefire-fails-shelling-resumes-and-hope-fades.

Spanger-Siegfried, Erika, Kristina Dahl, Astrid Caldas, and Shana Udvardy. "The US Military on the Front Lines of Rising Seas (2016)." *Union of Concerned Scientists*, www.ucsusa.org/global-warming/global-warming-impacts/sea-level-rise-flooding-us-military-bases#.WJU6RxiZM9U.

"Vaccines Do Not Cause Autism." *Centers for Disease Control and Prevention*, 23 Nov. 2015, www.cdc.gov/vaccinesafety/concerns/autism.html.

Always begin with the author when there is one. Reverse the first and last names of the first author only. When there are three or more, you may use just the first author and et al. Follow with the article title in quotation marks (periods and other terminal punctuation marks go inside closing quotation marks). Capitalize all words in titles except the following: articles, prepositions, coordinating conjunctions, and the "to" in infinitives unless they are the first or last words of a title or subtitle. Follow with the website name in italics. Follow

◀ KEYS TO THE EXERCISES ▶

with the page posting date or last update when provided. End with the URL (dropping "http:/") unless your instructor has told you to simply use the word "web" instead of the URL.

Begin with the article title if there is no author given. Alphabetize these entries by the first important word of the title.

The MLA no longer recommends date of access unless your instructor prefers it. See format below.

Alternatives:

Works Cited

"East Aleppo: A Ceasefire Fails, Shelling Resumes, and Hope Fades." *Doctors without Borders*, 14 Dec. 2016, web. Accessed 5 Feb. 2017.

Spanger-Siegfried, Erika, et al. "The US Military on the Front Lines of Rising Seas (2016)." *Union of Concerned Scientists*, web. Accessed 5 Feb. 2017.

"Vaccines Do Not Cause Autism." *Centers for Disease Control and Prevention*, 23 Nov. 2015, web. Accessed 5 Feb. 2017.

WORKS CITED EXERCISE #14 KEY: A FEATURE FILM AND A DOCUMENTARY

Works Cited

Anderson, Paul Thomas, director. *The Master*. Performances Joaquin Phoenix, Philip Seymour Hoffman, and Amy Adams, JoAnne Sellar Productions, 2012.

Going Clear: Scientology and the Prison of Belief. Directed by Alex Gibney, Jigsaw Productions, 2015.

◀ PART SEVEN ▶

When you focus on a particular creator of a film in your paper, begin with that person's name, followed by the term describing his or her contribution. Follow with the film's title in italics and a period; other contributors if desired, preceded by the appropriate descriptive term and followed by a comma; the company, followed by a comma; and the year and a period. Capitalize all words in titles except the following: articles, prepositions, coordinating conjunctions, and the "to" in infinitives unless they are the first or last words of a title or subtitle.

When you focus on the film itself, begin with its title in italics and a period. Follow with the contributor or contributors you are focusing on, preceded by the appropriate descriptive term and followed by a comma; the company, followed by a comma; and the year and a period.

WORKS CITED EXERCISE #15 KEY: A YOUTUBE VIDEO AND A SERIES ON NETFLIX

Works Cited

Black Mirror. Created by Charlie Brooker, House of Tomorrow, 2016. *Netflix*.

BLC Theatre Presents Hamlet by *William Shakespear*e. Directed by Peter Bloedel, uploaded by BLA Productions, 20 Aug. 2013. YouTube, www.youtube.com/watch?v=zz6GL6AFphU.

Bosch. Developed by Eric Overmeyer, Amazon, 2015-2016. Amazon Prime.

When focusing on the work, begin with that. Capitalize all words in titles except the following: articles, prepositions, coordinating conjunctions, and the "to" in infinitives unless they are the first or last words of a title or subtitle. Italicize films and videos. Add the contributors you are including, such as directors, preceded by the correct descriptors. For a series, follow with the production company and the year(s) of production for the series. That ends the first "container," so follow it with a period, and add the name of the next "container," such as the online subscription services Netflix and Amazon Prime. For a video from a site that you can access directly, follow the contributor you

◀ KEYS TO THE EXERCISES ▶

have included with the production company and with the uploader's name if provided. Since in this example the company and the uploader are the same, we do not need to supply the name twice. Follow that with the date uploaded. That ends the first "container," so use a period and then add the name of the next "container," such as YouTube, and then the URL (or the word "web" if your instructor prefers it. Always ask).

PART EIGHT

WORKSHEETS

◀ WORKSHEETS ▶

Name: _____

Worksheet 1: MLA Page Layout Exercise #1

Directions: Below is a sample of the top section of an MLA document. Circle or highlight any errors you see where the student failed to follow proper MLA format. If there are errors you cannot simply circle, explain them below.

                                                                    Mandvi pg. 1

Adira Mandvi

English 101

Professor Schmidt

4-3-17

                    Symbolism in the Stories of Angela Carter

The symbolism in Angela Carter's short stories based on classic fairy tales is both powerful and complex. An analysis of the three stories in her collection

Additional Errors:

◀ PART EIGHT ▶

Name: _____

Worksheet 2: MLA Page Layout Exercise #2

Directions: Below is a sample of the top section of an MLA document. Circle or highlight any errors you see where the student failed to follow proper MLA format. If there are errors you cannot simply circle, explain them below.

                                                                             Vasquez 1

Xochitl Vasquez

Professor Walter Bishop

Physics 102

Feb. 13th, 2017

<u>Physics and History</u>

The discipline we know as physics is the branch of science that developed out of the study of both philosophy and nature. It was called "natural philosophy"

Additional Errors:

◀ WORKSHEETS ▶

Name: _____

WORKSHEET 3: MLA PAGE LAYOUT EXERCISE #3

Directions: Below is a sample of the top section of an MLA document. Circle or highlight any errors you see where the student failed to follow proper MLA format. If there are errors you cannot simply circle, explain them below.

                                                                  Hoshiro

Wako Hoshiro

Winifred Burkle

Philosophy 1B

9 March 2017

                              Descartes Before The Horse

There is an old joke that was probably made up by either a philosophy professor or a philosophy student. A horse walks into a bar. The bartender

Additional Errors:

◀ PART EIGHT ▶

Name: _____

Worksheet 4: MLA Page Layout Exercise #4

Directions: Below is a sample of the top section of an MLA document. Circle or highlight any errors you see where the student failed to follow proper MLA format. If there are errors you cannot simply circle, explain them below.

Amy Pond

Professor Tennant

November 10, 2017

Hist. B2

The Birth of Western Civilization

    The statement "The first human being who hurled an insult instead of a rock was the true founder of civilization" was popularized by the father of

Additional Errors:

◀ WORKSHEETS ▶

Name: _____

Worksheet 5: MLA Page Layout Questions

Directions: Write the answer and the page number on which you found the answer.

Question 1: In the proper order, list the four key elements for the personal and class identification heading that goes in the upper-left corner of your first page.

Answer:

Question 2: How many spaces does MLA recommend that you use after terminal punctuation marks?

Answer:

Question 3: What information goes in the paper's header in the upper-right corner of every page?

Answer:

Question 4: True or false: You should have an extra space between each paragraph for clarity.

Answer: True   False

Question 5: Your margins should be what size on all four sides of the paper?

Answer:

◀ PART EIGHT ▶

Question 6: What line spacing should you use throughout your entire paper?

Answer:

Question 7: What is justification, and how does MLA say your paper should be justified?

Answer:

Question 8: Where does your paper's title go? How is it set off differently from the body?

Answer:

Question 9: Give an example of how MLA says to list the date you on which you submit your paper in your personal and class identification heading:

Answer:

Question 10: What size should the indentations be for each new paragraph in your paper?

Answer:

◀ WORKSHEETS ▶

Name: _____

Worksheet 6: Parentheticals In-Text Citations Questions

Directions: Write the answer and the page number on which you found the answer.

Question 1: When do you need to use in-text citations in your papers? Explain.

Answer:

Question 2: What do you put in an in-text citation for a work by a single author that includes page numbers when you have not mentioned the author's name before the material you have used? Explain and provide an example.

Answer:

Question 3: What do you put in an in-text citation for a work by a single author that includes page numbers when you have mentioned the author's name before the material you have used? Explain and provide an example.

Answer:

Question 4: Where do you place the period in relation to the in-text citation for a direct quotation under four lines? Explain and provide an example.

Answer:

Question 5: What do you use in an in-text citations when no author's name is provided? Explain and provide an example.

Answer:

◀ PART EIGHT ▶

Question 6: What do you put in an in-text citation for a work by two authors that includes page numbers when you have not mentioned the authors' names before the material you have used? Explain and provide an example.

Answer:

Question 7: What do you put in an in-text citation for a work by a three or more authors that includes page numbers when you have not mentioned the authors' names before the material you have used? Explain and provide an example.

Answer:

Question 8: What do you put in a sentence leading up to a quotation when your source quotes from another work and you use that quotation in your paper? What do you put in the in-text citation? Explain and provide an example.

Answer:

Question 9: What do you put in the in-text citations for works by different people with the same last name? Explain and provide examples.

Answer:

Question 10: How does the format for direct quotations four lines or under in your papers differ from the format for direct quotations four lines and over in your text? And where do you place the period in relation to the in-text citation? Explain

Answer:

◀ WORKSHEETS ▶

Name: _____

Worksheet 7: Parenthetical In-Text Exercise #1

Directions: Below is a list of variations that you might encounter while using in-text parenthetical citations. For each question below, respond by writing a sentence that includes an actual example of a sentence the way it might appear in a paper, complete with the proper type of citation. Feel free to make up a quotation, author, or title of source. This is meant to practice basics of MLA format, not research itself.

Write a sample sentence that includes a direct quotation and shows a parenthetical citation for the following variations. Assume each source below is in print and has page numbers to include.

Question 1: A book by one author.

Question 2: A book by two authors.

Question 3: A book by three or more authors.

Question 4: A book with no listed author.

Question 5. A scholarly article with no listed author.

◀ PART EIGHT ▶

Name: _____

Worksheet 8: Parenthetical In-Text Exercise #2

Directions: Below is a list of variations that you might encounter while using in-text parenthetical citations. For each question below, respond by writing a sentence that includes an actual example of a sentence the way it might appear in a paper, complete with the proper type of citation. Feel free to make up a quotation, author, or title of source. This is meant to practice basics of MLA format, not research itself.

Write a sample sentence that includes a direct quotation and shows a parenthetical citation for the following variations. Unless indicated, assume each source below is in print and has page numbers to include.

Question 1: A scholarly journal article with the author's name provided but no page numbers.

Question 2: An eBook

Question 3: Two or more authors with the same last name (provide two sentences, one for each author and source).

Question 4: Information from a film.

Question 5: A source quoting another work.

◀ WORKSHEETS ▶

Name: _____

Worksheet 9: Parenthetical In-Text Exercise #3

Directions: Below is a list of variations that you might encounter while using in-text parenthetical citations. For each question below, respond by writing a sentence that includes an actual example of a sentence the way it might appear in a paper, complete with the proper type of citation. Feel free to make up a quotation, author, or title of source. This is meant to practice basics of MLA format, not research itself.

Write a sample sentence that includes a direct quotation and shows a parenthetical citation for the following variations. Unless indicated, assume each source below is in print and has page numbers to include.

Question 1: A scholarly journal article that has no page numbers but includes paragraph numbers.

Question 2: More than one work by the same author (this will include two sentences, one for each source from the author).

Question 3: A video found on a website, such as YouTube

Question 4: A website

Question 5: A block quotation from a book by one author.

◀ PART EIGHT ▶

◀ WORKSHEETS ▶

Name: _____

Worksheet 10: Works Cited Questions #1

Directions: Write the answer and the page number on which you found the answer.

Question 1. How do you determine in what order to put your sources on your paper's works cited page?

Answer:

Question 2. What do you title your works cited page, and where do you put this title?

Answer:

Question 3. How should the lines of works cited entries be indented?

Answer:

Question 4. How do you format the title of a book, play, film, TV series, or website?

Answer:

Question 5. How do you format the name of a periodical (journal, magazine, or newspaper)?

Answer:

Question 6. How do you format the title of an article, essay, short story, poem, or TV episode?

Answer:

Question 7. What should precede page numbers in a works cited entry when you have both first and last page numbers?

Answer:

Question 8. What should precede page numbers in a works cited entry when the work is on only one page?

Answer:

Question 9. What do you do when a work in a periodical is on discontinuous pages?

Answer:

Question 10. How do you present the page numbers of a source when the first and last page numbers are within the same range of a hundred?

Answer:

◀ WORKSHEETS ▶

Name: _____

Worksheet 11: Works Cited Questions #2

Directions: Write the answer and the page number on which you found the answer.

Question 1. What do you do when you have a source that has no author provided? What comes first in that entry, and where do you place it in relation to other sources?

Answer:

Question 2. How do you begin the entries when you have multiple works by the same author on a works cited page?

Answer:

Question 3. How do you determine the order of the entries when you have multiple works by the same author on a works cited page?

Answer:

Question 4. How do you present the names of the authors of a work when there are two?

Answer:

Question 5. How does the Modern Language Association (MLA) prefer you to present the names of the authors of a work when there are three or more?

Answer:

Question 6. How many works-cited entries will you have if you have only one work from a particular anthology?

Answer:

Question 7. How many works-cited entries will you have if you have three works from a single anthology?

Answer:

Question 8: What are the four elements in each of an anthology's cross-referenced entries?

Answer:

Question 9: How do you usually set off subtitles from titles?

Answer:

Question 10. What are the exceptions to the way you usually set off subtitles from titles?

Answer:

◀ WORKSHEETS ▶

Name: _____

Worksheet 12: Works Cited Questions #3

Directions: Write the answer and the page number on which you found the answer.

Question 1. You should not capitalize the first letters of what parts of speech in the titles of your entries on works cited pages?

Answer:

Question 2. Where do commas and periods go in relation to closing quotation marks in works cited entries?

Answer:

Question 3. When you have two or more authors or editors of a work, in what order in an entry should their names go?

Answer:

Question 4. What types of words and abbreviations are omitted when you provide the names of book publishers? How would you present the following two publishers? (1) Woodbridge Company Ltd. and (2) McGraw Hill Education.

Answer:

◀ PART EIGHT ▶

Question 5. How do you handle the names of publishers when they are university presses? How would you present the following two publishers? (1) Yale University Press and (2) University Press of Maryland Press.

Answer:

Question 6. While you usually do not need to present the cities of publications for books in works cited entries any more, what situation provides an exception to this?

Answer:

Question 7. What does the MLA let you do when a book or play was published significantly earlier than the copy that you have?

Answer:

Question 8. How do you present volume and issue numbers for journal articles? Give an example.

Answer:

Question 9. When you use a periodical article from a library's database, how do you format the name of the database?

Answer:

Question 10. What does the MLA prefer at the very end of an entry for a journal article from a database?

Answer:

◀ WORKSHEETS ▶

Name: _____

Worksheet 13: Works Cited Entries #1

Directions: Highlight or underline the errors in the following works cited entries for books, and then explain how they should be fixed. If there are errors that cannot be easily circled or highlighted, discuss them.

Works Cited

Zipes, Jack. "The Irresistible Fairy Tale: The Cultural And Social History." Princeton: Princeton University Press, 2013.

Zipes, Jack. "The Brothers Grimm: From Enchanted Forests To The Modern World."Basingstoke: Palgrave Macmillan, 2002.

Giddens, Anthony, Mitchell Duneier, Richard P. Appelbaum, and Deborah Carr. "Introduction to Sociology," W. W. Norton & Company; 2016.

Fulcher, James; John Scott. "Sociology," Oxford University Press, 2011.

Explanations:

◀ PART EIGHT ▶

Name: _____

Worksheet 14: Works Cited Entries #2

Directions: Highlight or underline the errors in the following works cited entries for works from anthologies, and then explain how they should be fixed. Notes: Beautiful Losers is the name of a novel, and Hallelujah is the name of a song. The editor of the Colbert book's name is Aaron Allen Schiller (Aaron is his first name). The "So" in the title of that book is functioning as an adverb, not a coordinating conjunctions.

Works Cited

Burns, Steven. "Politics In Beautiful Losers. *Leonard Cohen And Philosophy: Various Positions*. Holt, Jason, ed. Open Court Publishing Company, 2014, pp. 139-153.

Stone, Peter. "The Happy Memes Of Hallelujah." *Leonard Cohen And Philosophy: Various Positions*. Holt, Jason, ed. Open Court Publishing Company, 2014, pp. 241-252.

Gimble, Steven. "Formidable Opponent And The Necessity Of Moral Doubt." *Stephen Colbert and Philosophy: I Am Philosophy* (And So Can You!) Allen Schiller, Aaron, ed. Open Court Publishing Company, 2009, pp. 19-27.

Explanations:

◀ WORKSHEETS ▶

Name: _____

Worksheet 15: Works Cited Entries #3

Directions: Highlight or underline the errors in the following works cited entries for works from print and scholarly journals, and then explain how they should be fixed.

Works Cited

Diergarten, Anna Katharina; Möckel, Thomas; Nieding, Gerhild; Ohler, Peter. "The Impact Of Media Literacy On Children's Learning From Films And Hypermedia." Journal Of Applied Developmental Psychology. Jan. 2017, Vol. 48, p33-41.

Fedorov, Alexander; Levitskaya, Anastasia. "Media Literacy Function In Critical Blogs." European Researcher. 2015, Vol. 93 Issue 4, p331-334. 4p. Academic Search Premier. DOI: 10.13187/er.2015.93.331.

Explanations:

Worksheet 16: Works Cited Entries #4

Directions: Highlight or underline the errors in the following works cited entries for works from print and scholarly journals, and then explain how they should be fixed.

Works Cited

Diergarten, Anna Katharina; Möckel, Thomas; Nieding, Gerhild; Ohler, Peter. "The Impact Of Media Literacy On Children's Learning From Films And Hypermedia." Journal Of Applied Developmental Psychology. Jan. 2017, Vol. 48, p33-41.

Fedorov, Alexander; Levitskaya, Anastasia. "Media Literacy Function In Critical Blogs." European Researcher. 2015, Vol. 93 Issue 4, p331-334. 4p. Academic Search Premier. DOI: 10.13187/er.2015.93.331.

Explanations:

◀ WORKSHEETS ▶

Name: _____

Worksheet 17: Works Cited Entries #5

Directions: Highlight or underline the errors in the following works cited entries for works from a scholarly journal from a database, a print magazine, and a newspaper article published online, and then explain how they should be fixed. The Nation is a magazine. State Politics & Policy Quarterly is a journal. The New York Times is a newspaper.

Berman, Ari. "John Lewis's Fight for Voting Rights." *The Nation* 6/24/2013, Vol. 296, pp. 20-26.

Harada, Masataka. "The Voting Rights Act of 1965 and Strategic Policy Making in the South." *State Politics & Policy Quarterly*. Dec2012, Vol. 12 Issue 4, p456-482. 27p. Academic Search Premier. DOI: 10.1177/1532440012451979.

Hasen, Richard. "Turning the Tide on Voting Rights." *The New York Times* August 2, 2016, https://www.nytimes.com/2016/08/02/opinion/campaignstops/turning-the-tide-on-voting-rights.html?_r=0.

Explanations:

◀ PART EIGHT ▶

Name: _____

Worksheet 18: Works Cited Entries #6

Directions: Highlight or underline the errors in the following works cited entries for works from a magazine article published online, a feature film, and a documentary, and then explain how they should be fixed. In each case, the focus is on the director.

Works Cited

Selma, directed by Ava DuVernay, 2014, Paramount Pictures.

Edelman, Ezra, Dir. O.J.: *Made in America*, ESPN Films, 2016.

Sheffield, Rob. "What O.J.: Made In America' Says About America Right Now," Rolling Stone, June 29, 2016, http://www.rollingstone.com/tv/features/what-o-j-made-in-america-says-about-america-right-now-20160629.

Explanations:

◀ WORKSHEETS ▶

Name: _____

Worksheet 19: Sentence Combining Exercise #1

Directions: Underline dependent clauses once and independent clauses twice. Circle or highlight any punctuation errors and supply corrections. If the sentence is correct, put a large C in the margin next to the number.

1. Many Americans love watching football and watch it throughout the season because it is so popular the Super Bowl in the US is the yearly championship game of the National Football League the Super Bowl is sometimes the most-watched American television broadcast of the year.

2. The 2016 Super Bowl broadcast drew an estimated 111.9 million viewers it was the third-most-watched broadcast in U.S. television history Americans love to watch the Super Bowl, and many even enjoy the commercials; they are often very imaginative, and they are sometimes controversial.

3. Football fans love to watch the Super Bowl game, and even enjoy the commercials, they are often very imaginative and sometimes controversial.

4. Because of the huge audience, commercial airtime is the most expensive of the year; the broadcast's commercials are even discussed in the media afterwards.

5. Super Bowl Sunday is extremely popular, so many Americans are glued to their TV sets most of that afternoon commercial airtime is the most expensive of the year during Super Bowl Sunday because of the huge audience.

6. American football is not without controversy brain damage was diagnosed in eighty-seven percent of donated brains of 202 football players in a 2017 study all but one of 111 brains of National Football League athletes had brain damage.

7. Many people in the United Kingdom and other countries love watching football and they watch it throughout the season, but it isn't what Americans call football.

8. Football is a popular sport in the United Kingdom and other countries but it is what Americans call soccer; it is played by approximately 250 million players in over 200 countries and dependencies, a "dependency" is a country or province controlled by another country.

9. Since soccer is played by approximately 250 million players in over 200 countries and dependencies it qualifies as the world's most popular sport.

◀ WORKSHEETS ▶

10. Soccer qualifies as the world's most popular sport because it is played by approximately 250 million players in over 200 countries and dependencies

11. Soccer is even more popular around the world than what Americans call football and most people in other countries think of soccer when they hear the word "football."

12. The Fédération Internationale de Football Association is commonly referred to simply as FIFA, it is an association governed by Swiss law; it was founded in 1904 and it is based in Zurich.

13. FIFA has over 200 member associations, and its official goal is the constant improvement of what it calls football and what Americans call soccer; the FIFA World Cup was first held in 1930 when FIFA president Jules Rimet decided to stage an international football tournament.

14. When FIFA president Jules Rimet decided to stage an international football tournament the first competition was held in 1930 the FIFA World Cup is the largest single-event sporting competition in the world.

15. The FIFA World Cup competition ordinarily happens every four years because of World War 11 the World Cup competition was not held in 1942 and 1946 competition resumed with the 1950 World Cup in Brazil.

Worksheet 20: Sentence Combining Exercise #2

Directions: Underline dependent clauses once and independent clauses twice. Circle or highlight any punctuation errors and supply corrections. If the sentence is correct, put a large C in the margin next to the number.

1. Reporters Without Borders is an international organization that promotes and defends freedom of information and freedom of the press; it has two main areas of activity, one is focused on Internet censorship and news media, and the other on providing assistance to journalists working in dangerous areas.

2. Reporters Without Borders announced the first International Online Free Expression Day in 2008, it is now called the World Day against Cyber Censorship.

3. Every year Reporters Without Borders compiles what it calls the World Press Freedom Index its 2017 Index "reflects a world in which attacks on the media have become commonplace and strongmen are on the rise."

4. Democracies began falling in the Index in the years before 2017 and Reporters Without Borders says that "nothing seems to be checking that fall." The United States fell two places, it ranked number forty-three in 2017; the United Kingdom also fell two places it ranked number forty in 2017.

◀ WORKSHEETS ▶

5. The organization described "a highly toxic anti-media discourse that drove the world into a new era of post-truth, disinformation, and fake news." It also said that "media freedom has retreated wherever the authoritarian strongman model has triumphed."

6. The country that ranked top in the 2017 World Press Freedom Index is Norway, and the country that ranked the lowest is North Korea.

7. Because even listening to a foreign radio broadcast can lead to a stay in a concentration camp North Koreans live in both ignorance and terror.

8. North Koreans live in both ignorance and terror since even listening to a foreign radio broadcast can lead to a stay in a concentration camp

9. Because Project Censored is an American organization that educates students and the public about the importance of a truly free press for democratic self-government; it exposes and opposes censorship of the news.

10. Project Censored educates students and the public about the importance of a truly free press because it opposes censorship of the news media it

publishes a book every year, the books report each year's twenty-five most ignored or censored independent news stories.

11. Anna Stepanovna Politkovskaya was a Russian journalist and human rights activist; she was known for her opposition to the policies of Vladimir Putin it was her reporting from Chechnya during the 1999-2005 Second Chechen War that made Politkovskaya's international reputation.

12. Dangers to Russian reporters have been well known since the early 1990s but concern at the number of killings rose after Anna Politkovskaya's murder in 2006 she was found dead in the elevator in her apartment building she had been shot four times at point-blank range.

13. She was murdered when she went into the elevator in her apartment building, but it is still unclear who paid for the killing that five men were later convicted of, her colleagues have protested that until the instigator of the crime is identified and prosecuted, the case is not closed.

14. December 15 is the "Remembrance Day of Journalists Killed on the Line of Duty in the Russian Federation"; when the Remembrance Day is observed every year, it does not get a lot of official attention in Russia.

15. The "Remembrance Day of Journalists Killed on the Line of Duty in the Russian Federation" does not get a lot of official attention in Russia, when it is observed.

Worksheet 21: Punctuating Independent Clauses, Dependent Clauses, and Phrases

Directions: In the following sentences, underline independent clauses twice and dependent clauses once and supply commas, semicolons, or periods where needed. Write C in the margin by any sentence that is correct as it is.

1. Angela Carter was an English novelist and journalist and she was most known for her magic realist novels and short stories.

2. Carter also contributed many articles to *The Guardian* a newspaper *The Independent* another newspaper and *New Statesman* a magazine.

3. Although she was known as a prolific writer of fiction Carter also contributed many articles to *The Guardian* *The Independent* and *New Statesman* they were later collected in a collection called *Shaking a Leg*.

4. She wrote many essays and articles even though she was most known for her fiction.

5. She was known as a prolific writer of fiction but she also contributed many articles to newspapers and magazines.

◀ PART EIGHT ▶

6. Carter accepted a commission to translate Charles Perrault's fairy tales from French into English in 1976 after the Perrault volume was published she embarked on the stories that were published in *The Bloody Chamber and Other Stories* with her reconceived versions of the stories collected by Perrault and the Brothers Grimm.

7. Her stories included versions of "Little Red Riding Hood" with werewolves and "Beauty and the Beast" with surprising transformations her reconception of "Puss in Boots" is a humorous and slightly ribald story reminiscent of a fabliau.

8. She adapted a number of her short stories for radio and wrote two original radio dramas on Richard Dadd and Ronald Firbank she collaborated with director Neil Jordan on the screenplay for *The Company of Wolves* it was based on three of her short stories.

9. She was also actively involved in the film adaptation of her novel *The Magic Toyshop* an adaption for the stage was written by Alan Harris and directed by Sita Calertt-Ennals.

10. *Nights at the Circus* is a novel by Carter that won the 1984 James Tait Black Memorial Prize for fiction it focuses on the life and exploits of Sophie Fevvers she claims to have been hatched from an egg and about to develop wings she performs as an aerialist.

◀ WORKSHEETS ▶

11. *Nights at the Circus* was adapted for the stage by Tom Morris and Emma Rice in 2006 for Kneehigh Theatre Company and it was performed in London before it toured other cities in England.

12. Angela Carter died at the age of fifty-one at her home in London after developing lung cancer at the time of her death Carter had started work on a sequel to Charlotte Brontë's *Jane Eyre*.

13. Her obituaries in the British press received more space than that of most celebrities who died that year she was considered one of the most important writers at work in the English language.

14. When her death was announced the publishing house with which her name was most closely associated sold out of her books within three days.

15. The British Academy received forty proposals for doctoral research into her work over the course of the next academic year this was in comparison with only three on the literature of the entire 18th century.

◀ PART EIGHT ▶

Name: _____

Worksheet 22: Punctuating Nonrestrictive Elements

Directions: Underline or highlight the nonrestrictive elements and punctuate them appropriately. Remember—nonrestrictive elements may contain information that is important to a piece of writing, but you can remove them from sentences without changing the actual meaning of the sentence.

1. The majority of Americans no matter what generation they belong to combine a mixture of sources and technologies for their news each every week according to a survey by the Media Insight Project.

2. According to a survey by the Media Insight Project an initiative of the American Press Institute and the Associated Press-NORC Center for Public Affairs Research where people go to get news depends on both the topic of the stories and on their nature.

3. The findings of the nationally representative telephone survey which involved 1,492 adults seem to challenge the idea of the so-called "filter bubble."

4. United States residents aged sixty and over are somewhat more likely than adults between the ages of eighteen and twenty-nine to say they enjoy staying current with the news.

◀ WORKSHEETS ▶

5. Older Americans who were classified as aged sixty and over are somewhat more likely to say they enjoy staying current with the news than the youngest cohort of Americans who were classified as adults between the ages of eighteen and twenty-nine.

6. Age does not seem to have an impact on people's attentiveness to different types of serious news topics such as politics and foreign affairs as both older and younger adults are interested in these issues.

7. Entertainment news which focuses on the entertainment business and its products is the only topic followed by a majority of younger people and a minority of older people.

8. Older adults turn more often to television radio and print media for their news than do younger adults who depend more on mobile devices.

9. Some younger adults are also more likely to favor social media which are far less reliable news sources than older adults.

10. The findings of the nationally representative telephone survey seem to challenge the idea of the so-called "filter bubble."

11. The "filter bubble" the notion that people follow only a few subjects in which they are interested and only from sources with which they agree was challenged by the study.

12. The study indicated that three-quarters of Americans pay attention to some news at least once a day including six out of ten people under the age of thirty.

13. The average American adult uses four of five different devices such as computers and cell phones for the news that they choose to consume on a daily basis.

14. The survey was designed to determine whether people distinguish between a reporting source the news organization that gathers the news from the means used to discover the news such as print publications or mobile phones.

15. The findings suggest that we make conscious choices about where we get our news and how we get it and that we use whatever technology is convenient at the moment.

WORKSHEET 23: Commas, Semicolons, Colons, and Periods Exercise #1

Directions: Identify independent clauses, dependent clauses, phrases, and nonrestrictive elements..

1. The original folktales told by peasants are very different from the versions that children today read or encounter in movies they often involve extreme violence and have unhappy endings.

2. Because they often involve extreme violence and have unhappy endings the original folktales told by peasants are very different from the versions that children today read or encounter in movies.

3. Early folktales sometimes dealt with the following issues incest cannibalism murder and parental abandonment of children.

4. Folktales are categorized into "tale types" based on motifs that they share the individual stories within a tale type are called "variants."

5. Folktales are categorized into "tale types" based on motifs that they share and the individual stories within a tale type are called "variants."

6. Folktales are categorized into "tale types" based on motifs that they share however the individual variants may contain significant differences.

7. Folktales are categorized into "tale types" based on motifs that they share the individual variants however may contain significant differences.

8. When we talk about folklore the term "motifs" refers to recurrent elements that create recognizable patterns in different stories common folkloric motifs include the heroine persecuted by a stepmother and children who outsmart an ogre or wolf who wishes to devour them.

9. Stories within a tale type may seem very different on the surface the tale type that contains "Beauty and the Beast" also contains "The Dog Bride" "The Pig King" and "The Frog Price, or Iron Heinrich."

10. The tale type that contains "Beauty and the Beast" also contains these variants "The Dog Bride" which ends with a man hanging himself "The Pig King" where the prince kills his first two wives and "The Frog Price, or Iron Heinrich" where the princess is an ill-tempered brat.

11. Although these three variants vary widely across cultures they still belong to the same tale type because they share the same basic motifs including an enchanted man who transforms into a human being due to the attentions of a woman.

12. Folktales have inspired many literary works Angela Carter's *The Bloody Chamber and Other Stories* is a collection of short stories using characters and elements from classic fairy tales however Carter's stories are very original and intended for adult readers.

13. Even though they are inspired by folklore we do not categorize literary works which are works that have individual authors as variants of tale types writers of literary fairy tales include Hans Christian Anderson and Oscar Wilde.

14. Hans Christian Andersen created his own stories and characters which are usually much darker than people who know his stories only from children's books or film adaptations realize he did not depend on classic fairy tales for his plots.

15. Oscar Wilde most famous as a playwright also wrote a number of enduring literary fairy tales such as "The Selfish Giant" some were intended primarily for children but others were better suited as satires that adults would understand Wilde is also known for the novel *The Picture of Dorian Gray* which has an element of fantasy.

Name: _____

Worksheet 24: Commas, Semicolons, Colons, and Periods Exercise #2

Directions: Identify independent clauses, dependent clauses, phrases, and nonrestrictive elements.

1. Bob Dylan who was born Robert Allen Zimmerman in 1941 is an American singer songwriter and writer and he has been influential in both popular music and popular culture for over five decades.

2. A contemporary of Dylan Leonard Cohen was born in 1934 he was a Canadian singer songwriter musician poet and novelist.

3. Cohen's work mainly explores the themes of isolation relationships religion and politics his most famous song is "Hallelujah" which has been covered by hundreds of singers.

4. Cohen's work mainly explores the following themes isolation relationships religion and politics.

5. In 2016 Bob Dylan was awarded the Nobel Prize for literature which sparked controversy among novelists musicians and fans.

6. Although Bob Dylan is more famous than Cohen Cohen's work was considered by many critics to be superior to Dylan's.

7. A number of commentators claimed that Cohen would have been a more appropriate choice when Dylan's Nobel Prize was announced but Cohen graciously applauded Dylan's honor.

8. The evening the award was announced Cohen performed in front of an audience in Los Angeles and remarked that Dylan receiving the award was like "pinning a medal on Mount Everest for being the highest mountain."

9. Joni Mitchell a contemporary of Dylan and Cohen is also known for her music and lyrics *Rolling Stone* called her "one of the greatest songwriters ever."

10. Younger generations are discovering the works of Bob Dylan born in 1941 Leonard Cohen born in 1934 and Joni Mitchell born in 1943.

11. The Woodstock Festival was a music festival in 1969 which attracted an audience of over 400,000 it was billed as "An Aquarian Exposition: 3 Days of Peace & Music" and it was held at Max Yasgur's 600-acre dairy farm in the Catskill Mountains it became the world's most famous musical event.

12. As musicians from around the country headed to Woodstock in August of 1969 Joni Mitchell was not among them she was scheduled to perform on *The Dick Cavett Show* the day after the festival ended and her agent her not to go because he was afraid she would miss the show.

13. Her biographer David Yaffe wrote that Mitchell was bitterly disappointed to miss Woodstock she wrote the song "Woodstock" which he says held tremendous emotional weight for her stating that "the lyrics are not really a celebration especially when you hear the way she sings it it's a dirge."

14. Mitchell wrote "Woodstock" in a hotel room in New York City while she watched televised reports of the festival singer David Crosby said that "Woodstock" managed to capture both the feeling and importance of the festival better than anyone who had actually been there.

15. The group Crosby, Stills, Nash and Young created a more upbeat musical arrangement when they covered "Woodstock" it was released as the lead single from their 1970 *Déjà Vu* album it has been covered many times since by a wide variety of singers and groups in a wide variety of styles.

◀ WORKSHEETS ▶

Name: _____

Worksheet 25: Commas, Semicolons, Colons, and Periods Exercise #3

Directions: Identify independent clauses, dependent clauses, phrases, and nonrestrictive elements.

1. Alfred Nobel was a Swedish industrialist and inventor he held 355 patents and became a wealthy man it was Nobel's construction work that inspired him to research new methods of blasting rock so he started experimenting with an explosive substance called nitroglycerin.

2. Because he was interested in developing new methods of blasting rock he started working with an explosive chemical substance called nitroglycerin.

3. He became interested in experimenting with nitroglycerin twenty years after it was invented by an Italian chemist it is very volatile in its liquid state and he discovered that mixing it with silica produced what he called "dynamite."

4. Nobel stipulated in his last will and testament that 94% of his total assets go toward the creation of an endowment fund to honor achievements that benefitted humanity and one of the annual prizes is the Nobel Peace Prize.

5. When it was revealed that he had established a special peace prize it created an international sensation his name was connected with explosives and with inventions useful to making war it was not connected to peace.

6. Bertha von Suttner was an Austrian pacifist and novelist she was the first woman to be solely awarded the Nobel Peace Prize becoming the second female Nobel laureate after Marie Curie's 1903 award von Suttner won her award in 1905.

7. Suttner's Nobel lecture which was delivered in 1906 was titled "The Evolution of the Peace Movement" and it is posted on *NobelPrize.org* the official website of the Nobel Prize.

8. Bertha von Suttner was a countess and a friend of Alfred Nobel Suttner became a leading figure in the Austrian peace movement with the publication her pacifist novel *Lay Down Your Arms*.

9. *Lay Down Your Arms* whose German name is *Die Waffen Nieder* was published in thirty-seven editions and was translated into a dozen languages Suttner also gained international respect as the editor of an international pacifist journal that was named after her novel.

10. Suttner took part in the organization of the First Hague Conventions in 1899 the Hague Conventions were a series of international treaties and declarations that were negotiated at two peace conferences in The Hague a city on the western coast of the Netherlands.

11. Although Suttner's personal contact with Alfred Nobel was relatively brief they corresponded until his death in 1896 and it is widely believed that Suttner was a major influence in his decision to include a peace prize among the prizes provided in his will.

12. Nobel's ideas about war and peace were written down during his years of correspondence with Suttner Nobel wrote "on the day that two army corps can mutually annihilate each other in a second all civilized nations will surely recoil with horror and disband their troops."

13. After Nobel established his dynamite factories he told von Suttner that he hoped they would help put an end to war because he thought that nations would "surely recoil with horror" at dynamite's power to annihilate cities.

14. Because Nobel thought that nations would "surely recoil with horror" at dynamite's power to annihilate cities he hoped that his dynamite factories would help put an end to war unfortunately he was very wrong.

15. Suttner was an important force in the international peace movement and she tried to get Nobel to engage himself in this activity Nobel did not live long enough to see the First World War and discover how wrong his ideas about the deterrent effects of dynamite were.

◀ WORKSHEETS ▶

Name: _____

Worksheet 26: Commas, Semicolons, Colons, and Periods Exercise #4

Directions: Identify independent clauses, dependent clauses, phrases, and nonrestrictive elements.

1. "Confirmation bias" is the tendency to interpret new evidence as confirmation of existing beliefs this contributes to overconfidence in personal beliefs and can allow people to maintain beliefs in the face of evidence that disproves them.

2. Confirmation bias is also known as "my-side bias" and "confirmatory bias" two people with opposing views on a topic can see the same evidence however they may both believe that this evidence values their own views.

3. Failing to interpret information in an unbiased way can lead to serious errors in judgment we need to learn how to identify it in ourselves and in other people one important step is to be cautious of the way that we interpret data that seems to immediately support our own views.

4. In a Stanford University study half of the participants were in favor of capital punishment and the other half were opposed to it both groups were given details of the same two fictional studies however the groups were told different things about what the studies proved.

5. Half the participants were told that one study supported the deterrent effect of capital punishment and the other study opposed it the other half of the participants were given the opposite information.

6. At the conclusion of the Stanford study the majority of the participants maintained their original views pointing only to the data that supported these views and ignoring the data that undercut their views.

7. The word "literacy" has traditionally referred to the ability to read and write these days however we get most of our information through a variety of media technologies media literacy is defined as the ability to successfully and objectively access analyze and evaluate media.

8. More and more people these days get their news either primarily or entirely online so media literacy has become more important than ever different ideas can be consumed as if they were real journalism including opinions poorly understood interpretations of the news and actual lies.

9. Ideas that can be consumed as if they were examples of real journalism include the following opinions poorly understood interpretations of the news and actual lies.

10. Examples of things that are not real journalism include opinions which are views formed that are not always based on facts poorly-understood interpretations of news stories which may not be deliberately dishonest and actual lies which may be intended to cause damage.

11. Fake news is not a twenty-first century phenomenon alone historian Robert Darnton writes that "the circulation of mendacious rumors many of them in songs and poems no longer than today's tweets led to [. . .] a transformation of the political landscape in April 1749."

12. Although fake news is not a twenty-first century phenomenon alone twenty-first century technology has made it far more widespread and dangerous social media provide both malicious and naïve individuals the opportunity to disseminate a great deal of fake news.

13. Fake news is not a twenty-first century phenomenon alone even though twenty-first century technology has made it far more widespread and dangerous.

14. Rumors and misinformation can spread quickly through social media outlets including Twitter and Facebook false information from social media is especially dangerous because it spreads so quickly potentially influencing millions of users.

15. A vital part of media literacy means learning how to recognize confirmation bias in ourselves and others seeking the truth needs to take precedence in simply feeling right and maintaining the beliefs that make us most comfortable a good start is exposing ourselves to a variety of news sources and analyzing evidence objectively.

◀ WORKSHEETS ▶

Name: _____

Worksheet 27: Commas, Semicolons, Colons, and Periods Exercise #5

Directions: Identify independent clauses, dependent clauses, phrases, and nonrestrictive elements.

1. L. Frank Baum who wrote *The Wonderful Wizard of Oz* and its sequels was the son-in-law of an early feminist Matilda Joslyn Gage her influence is felt throughout the Oz books because they focus on a courageous and intelligent girl.

2. L. Frank Baum's Dorothy is a sweet little girl who travels to another world far from Kansas this other world's existence was partly inspired by a real struggle for liberation.

3. The famous 1939 film turned a "real" adventure into a dream and it altered the original book's themes furthermore Dorothy is not a little girl in the film she is a teenager.

4. After 20th Century Fox refused to lend Shirley Temple a child actress to MGM Judy Garland a teenager was cast in the role.

5. Many works have been based on the Oz books including *Wizard of Oz* a 1939 film *Wicked: The Life and Times of the Wicked Witch of the West* a novel by Gregory Maguire and *A Barnstormer in Oz* a novel by Philip Jose Farmer.

6. Many works have been based on the Oz books, including the following *Wizard of Oz Wicked* and a series of books by Philip Jose Farmer.

7. In Maguire's *Wicked* the focus is on Elphaba who becomes the wicked witch the Wizard of Oz is in Maguire's *Wicked* too but he is an evil man he is not the bumbler portrayed in the Baum books and in the 1939 movie.

8. *Wicked* also became the basis for a Broadway musical with the same name the Broadway musical changes the plot of the book it was based on in many dramatic ways most members of the audience however enjoy the musical tremendously.

9. When *Wicked* was adapted for Broadway many plot and character changes were made but most members of the audience enjoy the musical tremendously.

10. Many major plot and character changes were made when *Wicked* was adapted into a popular and long-running Broadway musical.

11. Gregory Maguire wrote three other Oz-inspired books *Son of a Witch* about Elphaba's son *A Lion Among Men* about the "cowardly lion" and *Out of Oz* the final book in the series.

12. Gregory Maguire's Oz-inspired books are *Wicked: The Life and Times of the Wicked Witch of the West Son of a Witch A Lion Among Men* and *Out of Oz*.

13. In *Wicked: The Life and Times of the Wicked Witch of the West* Elphaba is initially a sympathetic character which is not what people would expect from the original book or any of the movie versions she is persecuted by many people because she was born with green skin.

14. Elphaba grows up to occupy many different roles including anti-totalitarian agitator animal-rights activist and nurse the Wizard of Oz is a dictator and the character of Dorothy is not introduced until nearly the end of the novel.

15. Philip Jose Framer's *A Barnstormer in Oz* takes place many years after the original Oz story the protagonist is Hank Stover who is a pilot and the son of Dorothy Gale he finds himself in Oz in 1923 after his plane gets lost in a green cloud over Kansas in 1923.

Name: _____

WORKSHEET 28: COMMAS, SEMICOLONS, COLONS, AND PERIODS EXERCISE #6

Directions: Identify independent clauses, dependent clauses, phrases, and nonrestrictive elements.

1. People typically think of short stories when they think of Raymond Carver he has been described as the most influential and important American short story writer since Ernest Hemingway but his death at the age of fifty ended his career early.

2. Carver's most anthologized works include the following "What We Talk about When We Talk about Love " "Cathedral" and "A Small, Good Thing."

3. When people think of Raymond Carver they typically think of his short fiction he was also however a well-regarded poet.

4. In the 1960s Carver and his family lived in Sacramento where he worked at a bookstore before taking a position as a night custodian at a hospital he rushed through his janitorial work every night so that he could write for the rest of his shift.

5. Carver audited classes at Sacramento State College and he took workshops with poet Dennis Schmitz Carver and Schmitz became friends and Carver wrote and published his first book of poetry titles *Near Klamath* with Schmitz's help.

6. 1967 was a landmark year for Carver because *Near Klamath* was published and one of his stories "Will You Please Be Quiet, Please?" was published in Martha Foley's annual *Best American Short Stories* anthology.

7. Carver's first short story collection *Will You Please Be Quiet, Please?* which was named after the story that appeared in Foley's anthology was published in 1976 the collection itself was shortlisted for the National Book Award.

8. Carver was nominated for the National Book Award again in 1984 for his third short story collection *Cathedral* many critics consider this his best collection like his other collections the title is taken from one of its stories.

9. Included in *Cathedral* are the title story and the award-winning stories "A Small, Good Thing" and "Where I'm Calling From."

10. Alejandro G. Iñárritu directed and co-wrote a film titled *Birdman or (The Unexpected Virtue of Ignorance)* which was usually referred to simply as *Birdman* after its release in 2014.

11. Carver's "What We Talk about When We Talk about Love" is featured in *Birdman* a film about a has-been actor who is producing a play based on this story Carver's words run throughout the film which begins with an excerpt from one of Carver's poems.

12. Elements in *Birdman* confused some viewers however fans who recognized these elements as stemming from the tradition of magic realism were not confused it is a literary genre that incorporates fantastic elements into otherwise realistic fiction.

13. Magic realism was originally associated with Latin American authors such as Jorge Luis Borges and Gabriel García Márquez yet writers from other cultures are also known for their magic realist works.

14. Writers from other cultures are also known for their magic realist works such as Angela Carter who is English Salman Rushdie who is British Indian and Toni Morrison who is North American.

15. Carver's work is highly realistic it is very different from the works of magical realist writers nevertheless Carver and magic realism are linked in *Birdman*.

WORKSHEET 29: COMMAS, SEMICOLONS, COLONS, AND PERIODS EXERCISE #7

Directions: Identify independent clauses, dependent clauses, phrases, and nonrestrictive elements.

1. Morgan Spurlock is a move producer director and writer and he has made several movies including *Super Size Me* released in 2004 *The Greatest Movie Ever Sold* released in 2011 and *Censored Voices* released in 2015.

2. He appears in one of his own movies *Super Size Me* is a about a month that Spurlock spent eating nothing but food from McDonald's as a result of this he gained over twenty-four pounds this resulted in a 13% body mass increase and a cholesterol level of 230 it took Spurlock fourteen months to lose the weight he gained.

3. Spurlock's rules included the following he had to eat three McDonald's meals per day he had to super size any meal when asked and he could not engage in more exercise than what is estimated for the average American.

4. Spurlock started the month with breakfast near his home in Manhattan where there is an average of four McDonald's locations per square mile he aimed to keep the distances he walked in line with the approximately two miles walked per day by the average American.

5. Day Two brought Spurlock's first of nine Super-Size meals the meal was a Double Quarter Pounder with Cheese Super Size French fries and a forty-two ounce Coke it took twenty-two minutes to eat.

6. After this meal Spurlock experienced steadily increasing stomach discomfort and he promptly vomited in the parking lot when he left the restaurant

three weeks later he had heart palpitations his internist advised him to stop the experiment to avoid serious health problems.

7. His doctor compared Spurlock to the protagonist in the film *Leaving Las Vegas* who drinks himself to death in a matter of weeks the doctor was surprised at the amount of deterioration in Spurlock's health after the month ended.

8. Other documentaries about food include *Forks Over Knives* which advocates a plant-based diet *Sugar Coated* which addresses the politics surrounding the sugar industry *Fed Up* which focuses on the staggering rates of obesity in the United States and *King Corn* which looks at the government's role in the mass industrialization of the corn farming industry.

9. Other documentaries about food include the following four *Forks Over Knives Sugar Coated Fed Up* and *King Corn*.

10. *Fast Food Nation* is a 2006 feature film that examines the health risks and environmental and social consequences involved in the fast food industry it was based on Eric Schlosser's best-selling work of investigative journalism *Fast Food Nation: The Dark Side of the All-American Meal*.

11. Schlosser's *Fast Food Nation* exposed how the fast food industry has widened the gap between rich and poor added to the exploitation of workers helped to cause an epidemic of obesity and altered food production around the world.

12. The feature film based on Schlosser's book addresses many of the same issues through interlocking stories that follow a variety of fictional characters including immigrants fast food restaurant workers and employees at a meat-packing plant.

◀ WORKSHEETS ▶

13. *Fast Food Nation* was directed by Richard Linklater the screenplay was written by Linklater and Schlosser and it won Best Feature Film at the 21st Genesis Awards Linklater was nominated for the Palme d'Or at the 2006 Cannes Film Festival.

14. *Fast Food Nation* was directed by Richard Linklater and the screenplay was written by Linklater and Schlosser it won Best Feature Film at the 21st Genesis Awards furthermore Linklater was nominated for the Palme d'Or at the 2006 Cannes Film Festival.

15. Although Linklater was nominated for the Palme d'Or at the 2006 Cannes Film Festival he did not win English director Ken Loach won the Palme d'Or with his movie *The Wind That Shakes the Barley*.

Worksheet 30: Commas, Semicolons, Colons, and Periods Exercise #8

Directions: Identify independent clauses, dependent clauses, phrases, and nonrestrictive elements.

1. The term "Cold War" does not refer to actual armed conflict it refers to the political and military tension after World War II between powers in the Eastern and Western Blocs.

2. When we hear about the Cold War we usually do not think of jazz musicians nonetheless they played a part.

3. During the Cold War the State Department launched a public relations campaign that it called the Jazz Ambassadors Program and it sent performers like Louis Armstrong and Duke Ellington on tours around the world the purpose was to help counter Soviet propaganda.

4. The State Department sent artists around the world including the following Louis Armstrong a trumpeter composer and singer Duke Ellington a composer pianist and bandleader Dave Brubeck a pianist and composer and Randy Weston also a pianist and composer.

5. Since those days the Bureau of Educational and Cultural Affairs in the United States State Department has sponsored the Jazz Ambassadors in partnership with the John F. Kennedy Center for the Performing Arts they also conduct master classes and lecture-recitals for local musicians in addition to performing public concerts.

◀ WORKSHEETS ▶

6. Sixty years after Randy Weston toured with the Jazz Ambassadors he released a new album called *The African Nubian Suite* he was ninety-one years old Weston was born April 6 1926 in Brooklyn the traditional music of Africa has influenced Weston's jazz since he first started writing and performing.

7. Weston's musical journey began in Brooklyn in the 1920s when it was racially segregated his parents told him that he was an "American-born African" and taught him to be proud of his heritage.

8. Weston has said "If you look at the piano inside is a harp a harp is one of the oldest African instruments when I touch the piano it becomes an African instrument it's no longer a European instrument I say that in a positive way not a negative way."

9. After serving in the United States Army during World War II, Weston ran a restaurant that was popular among leading bebop musicians bebop is a type of jazz that originated in the 1940s it was characterized by complex harmony and rhythms.

10. Bebop also called simply bop features songs characterized by a fast tempo rapid chord changes numerous changes of key instrumental virtuosity and improvisation.

11. Weston's musical heroes include Count Basie Nat King Cole Art Tatum and Duke Ellington but it was Thelonious Monk who had the greatest impact on his career and style.

12. Weston believes that cultures can build bridges through music and he incorporated an African influence into his compositions even before his first State Department tour in 1965.

13. Even before his first State Department tour in 1965 Randy Weston was incorporating an African influence into his compositions and performances.

14. Robin Kelley the author of a book that explores the influence of African music on jazz calls *The African Nubian Suite* a profound musical composition.

15. Weston celebrated his ninetieth birthday in 2016 with a concert at Carnegie Hall and continues to tour and speak internationally *The African Nubian Suite* was released in 2017.

◀ WORKSHEETS ▶

Name: _____

WORKSHEET 31: COMMAS, SEMICOLONS, COLONS, AND PERIODS EXERCISE #9

Directions: Identify independent clauses, dependent clauses, phrases, and nonrestrictive elements.

1. Frida Kahlo was born in 1907 in Coyocoán which is in Mexico City Kahlo is considered one of Mexico's greatest artists but she only began painting after she was badly injured in a bus accident.

2. After she was injured in an accident when she was eighteen Kahlo started painting she had been on her way home when the bus she was in collided with a streetcar Kahlo suffered nearly fatal injuries and fractured several ribs her legs and a collarbone.

3. Mexican culture is important in her work which has been called both naïve art and surrealist art André Breton who is considered the primary initiator of surrealism described her art as a "bomb wrapped in a ribbon."

4. Her father was a German emigrant and her mother was a native-born Mexican Kahlo said her father was the person who taught her about literature nature and philosophy.

5. Before she was injured in the accident she dreamed of becoming a doctor the accident ended the dream and caused her pain for the rest of her life.

6. Kahlo married Diego Rivera another artist his reputation grew before hers did but her paintings began to raise interest in the United States.

7. Each of these artists regarded the other as Mexico's greatest painter and Kahlo referred to Diego as the "architect of life" they were proud of each other's creations despite the fact that they were drastically different in style in fact their differences in style may have made their mutual admiration easier.

8. Diego who was a social realist is reported to have actually shed tears of pride when Picasso admired the eyes in one of Kahlo's paintings.

9. In 1941 her works were featured at the Institute of Contemporary Art in Boston and in 1942 she participated in two high-profile exhibitions in Manhattan the Twentieth-Century Portraits exhibition and the Surrealists' First Papers of Surrealism exhibition.

10. Kahlo was known for her brutally honest self-portraits they reveal her psychological response to physical pain and emotional adversity.

11. Kahlo was known for her brutally honest self-portraits because they reveal her psychological response to physical pain and emotional adversity.

12. *The Two Fridas* is a double self-portrait that Kahlo painted in 1939 and it is now one of her most recognized compositions she depicts herself in modern European attire and in traditional Mexican attire.

13. Kahlo's paintings include *The Two Fridas* a double self-portrait *Self-Portrait with Cropped Hair* depicting Kahlo as androgynous and *Fulang-Chang and I* a portrait with Fulang-Chang her pet spider monkey.

14. Kahlo's paintings include the following *The Two Fridas Self-Portrait with Cropped Hair* and *Fulang-Chang and I.*

15. When Frida Kahlo died at the age of forty-seven in 1954 she left paintings a collection of letters to lovers and friends and candid journal entries all of these mark her as a true original.

◀ WORKSHEETS ▶

Name: _____

Worksheet 32: Apostrophes, Plurals, and Pronouns Exercise #1

Directions: Circle or highlight and fix any errors that you see in the following sentences, changing spelling and adding or deleting apostrophes and the letter "s" as needed. Write C in the margin by any sentence that is correct as it is.

1. I'm afraid I don't know what the problems cause is.

2. All the athletes schedules were very busy. [Multiple athletes.]

3. Each athletes schedule was very busy.

4. The Costellos' have three daughters and two sons.

5. The Costellos' house is up for sale because they need to move to a bigger place.

6. Each childs personality is open and cheerful.

7. The childrens parents dote on them all.

8. Its never easy moving a large family from one house to another.

9. Alma's and Ivan's school projects' won a prize. [They worked together.]

10. Alma's and Ivan's houses are on the same block, which was convenient.

11. The firm employs several notary publics.

12. The dog chased it's tail until it got very dizzy.

13. I have at least two weeks worth of work to catch up on.

14. All my project's are demanding and take a lot of hour's to complete.

15. Can you put you're books back on the shelves?

16. Both my two sisters grades were better than mine were, so I was jealous of them.

17. A mother kangaroo carries' it's babies in it's pouch.

18. ochitl's sister-in-laws car is a hybrid. [She has only one sister-in-law.]

19. Rasheed's two sisters-in-laws cars are also hybrids; they love the mileage they get.

20. Whose car get's the best mileage?

◀ WORKSHEETS ▶

Name: _____

Worksheet 33: Apostrophes, Plurals, and Pronouns Exercise #2

Directions: Circle or highlight and fix any errors that you see in the following sentences, changing spelling and adding or deleting apostrophes and the letter "s" as needed. Write C in the margin by any sentence that is correct as it is.

1. Susans and Cathys apartment is small but attractive.

2. Johns and Melodys homes are next door to each other.

3. The childrens' toys' were scattered all over the floor.

4. The womens soccer team won all it's games.

5. Deborahs father-in-law hobby is bird watching.

6. Abe has two sister-in-law and their both doctors.

7. The two sister-in-law practices are demanding but satisfying.

8. You received Sam's birthday card, but did you get our's?

9. Did you see who stole that womans purse?

10. It was the same person who stole two mens wallets last week.

11. The tree has lost two of its lower branches.

12. Did you try to get somebody elses opinion?

13. Manuels cat, Camilla, is a "tuxedo cat"; his two dogs are spaniels.

14. The spaniels coats are spotted like Camillas.

15. Camilla had seven kittens three weeks after Manuel adopted her

16. All seven kittens eyes have just opened.

17. Next weeks meeting has been cancelled.

18. Megan has worked for several company's.

19. Megan's largely responsible for the company's successes. [Several different ones.]

20. Both girls' coats are in they're rooms.

◀ WORKSHEETS ▶

Name: _____

Worksheet 34: Apostrophes, Plurals, and Pronouns Exercise #3

Directions: Circle or highlight and fix any errors that you see in the following sentences, changing spelling and adding or deleting apostrophes and the letter "s" as needed. Write C in the margin by any sentence that is correct as it is.

1. I lost my camera, so I borrowed their's.

2. It's better to get a head start on a paper than to put it off till the day before.

3. Our teacher was pleased with everyones paper.

4. I don't know too much about they're new schedule.

5. The grizzly bear carefully protected it's lair.

6. This set of notes probably belongs to her.

7. The country has had many different Attorney General over the last few decades.

8. Each Attorney General approach is different.

9. Victoria's brother's are Luke and Joe, and they play on different team's.

10. Luke and Joe teams competed against each other.

11. They respect each other teams.

◀ PART EIGHT ▶

12. One teams record is slightly better than the other teams record.

13. Antonia is Sofia and Samuel sister-in-law.

14. We looked at one anothers photograph albums.

15. Her albums contents were impressive. [One album.]

16. Black cats are considered bad luck in some cultures.

17. A cats color may determine whether it is considered good luck or bad luck, depending on its culture.

18. Some of Halloweens symbols include black cats, Jack O'Lanterns, ghosts, witches, and vampires.

19. Bruce and Terri house is where we are going for Saturday nights Halloween party.

20. Its an annual tradition.

◀ WORKSHEETS ▶

Name: _____

Worksheet 35: Apostrophes, Plurals, and Pronouns Exercise #4

Directions: Circle or highlight and fix any errors that you see in the following sentences, changing spelling and adding or deleting apostrophes and the letter "s" as needed. Write C in the margin by any sentence that is correct as it is.

1. The traditional story lines of many classic fairy tales' differ from there original forms.

2. Cinderella and Snow White stepmothers were very wicked in every variant.

3. Sleeping Beautys prince didn't just kiss the princess in some variants'.

4. The Wilsons twin babies room was painted lilac.

5. Cindys mother-in-law offer to baby sit was appreciated.

6. The twins birthday is next month—they will be one year old.

7. Kristen and Sonya party was great.

8. Bruno and Elena papers were on the same topic, but their views were different.

9. The lawyers reputation was damaged by his ambulance chasing.

10. Lots of lawyers' aren't ambulance chasers.

11. She's a fan of both womens and mens sports.

12. That movies ending was unbelievable.

13. Few movies conclusions are that unusual.

14. I know your a fan of horror films—have you seen any good one's lately?

15. All the films' that are nominated for Oscars' this year are entreating. Didnt he say when he would arrive at Arnies house? [The name of his friend is Arnie.]

16. Its such a beautiful day that Ive decided to take a long walk.

17. She said the watch Jack found was hers, but she couldnt identify the manufacturers name on it.

18. Little girls clothing is on the first floor, and the boys department is on the second.

19. Erik's daughter-in-laws birthday is next week.

20. Joan has three daughter-in law.

◀ STUDENT NOTES ▶

◀ STUDENT NOTES ▶